Dream

LANGUAGE

JAMES W. *and* MICHAL ANN

GOLL

the prophetic power of dreams,
revelations, and the spirit of wisdom

Dream

LANGUAGE

DESTINY IMAGE® PUBLISHERS, INC.
P.O. Box 310, Shippensburg, PA 17257-0310

"Speaking to the Purposes of God for this Generation and for the Generations to Come."

This book and all other Destiny Image, Revival Press, Mercy Place, Fresh Bread, Destiny Image Fiction, and Treasure House books are available at Christian bookstores and distributors worldwide.

For a U.S. bookstore nearest you, call 1-800-722-6774.

For more information on foreign distributors, call 717-532-3040.

Or reach us on the Internet: www.destinyimage.com

ISBN 10: 0-7684-2354-6
ISBN 13: 978-0-7684-2354-9

For Worldwide Distribution, Printed in the U.S.A.

1 2 3 4 5 6 7 8 9 10 11 / 09 08 07 06

DEDICATION

To Jesus,

a Dream Come True!

With Gratefulness,

James W. and Michal Ann Goll

ENDORSEMENTS

James Goll tells his story of discovering God's dream for his life. You will find help in this book to understand and follow God's directions in your own life.

Billy Joe Daugherty
Victory Christian Center, Tulsa, OK

James Goll is a superb writer and he has delivered marvelously on a very pertinent topic for these days. The Bible has much to say about dreams and James helps put the whole topic into clear perspective for us.

Pat Williams
Senior Vice President
Orlando Magic

James and Michal Ann Goll have blessed us with vital truths and living examples to understand and fulfill dreams. The reader will discover the real purpose and meaning of dreams. Biblical and practical guidelines are given to help an individual discern whether the dream was divinely given and how to properly apply its meaning. James and Michal Ann, thanks for helping us to understand and fulfill our spiritual dreams.

Dr. Bill Hamon
Apostle, Bishop of Christian International Ministries Network

Francis Bacon said, "Reading maketh a full man speaking, a ready man; writing, an exact man." After reading James' book I would add... "and dreaming, a complete man." Those dreams I once dismissed now have meaning, and I have the prophetic guide, James Goll to thank. For God speaks in the language of image, symbol, color and sense and nobody does a better job of explaining the prophetic realm and its language than James Goll.

Dr. Lance Walnau
Lance Learning Group

Everyone is dreaming! It's just one of the languages of Heaven. If we are to interpret the signs and the times then we need master technicians to help us. It has been my great pleasure to know and work with James and Michal Ann Goll. I cannot think of anyone more spiritually prepared or experienced in the pragmatics of dream language than this couple. I have heard them teach on intrinsic and extrinsic dreams in particular... brilliant! That alone is worth the price of this book. If you're a dreamer then interpreting dream language is a must. This is a book that will put wings under the feet of the process that you need to move quickly into that new land of the Spirit that awaits.

Graham Cooke

TABLE OF CONTENTS

FOREWORD

My wife awakened me early one morning. Her first statement was, "I believe I have a warning for us... well, maybe it's a direction." She then began to explain a dream that she had during the night. She dreamed that she was standing in front of a huge mountain. She could not go over the mountain. She could not go through the mountain. Nor could she go around the mountain. In the dream she heard a voice saying, "Speak to this mountain and your way will open up." This dream and the revelation released through it have become very significant to us as we have journeyed through our 34 years of marriage. Many times we have seen our path close and we have remembered when God spoke and said, "Speak to this mountain and your way will open up."

When I lay down at night, I want to sleep in peace. I also want to be open for the Lord to reveal Himself and enlighten me to key information that I could not grasp during my busy, hectic day. Many times our sleep is the only time we are quiet and still enough for our creative Father to speak to us. James and Michal Ann Goll have written a book that is most helpful for us when we are awake to understand what was communicated to us when we were asleep. *Dream Language* is an excellent book to assist anyone—old or young, mature or immature—in understanding God's creative, mysterious communications at night. Not only is this a book that you can't quit reading, it is also a wonderful reference to assist you in interpreting what God is saying to you as He weaves together life changing revelation while you sleep.

A dream is a release of revelation (whether natural or spiritual) that comes at a time when your body is at peace and you are settled. Sometimes this is the only way God can communicate with you because your soul is quiet enough for the Lord to speak deeply into your spirit. A dream is like a snapshot of something you can relate to in picture form. Ecclesiastes 5:3 speaks of a dream coming when there are many cares. It may be a subconscious response to the circumstances of your life or the Holy Spirit communicating to you.

In the ancient eastern world, dreams were treated as reality. Dreams were considered to be the world of the divine or the demonic, and they often revealed the future. Dreams could be filled with revelation that would cause the dreamer to make the right decision for his or her future. Israel was forbidden to use many of the same type of divining practices as Egypt and other neighboring countries and peoples. However, God would visit them in the night to communicate His will and way to them. This continued throughout the Bible. In the first two chapters of the New Testament alone, God gave direction through prophetic dreams five times. We as Christians can receive revelation from dreams that are inspired by the Holy Spirit as well.

One of the reasons I love *Dream Language* is because not only does it teach you about dreams, but this book actually helps you in the process of remembering your dreams. James and Michal Ann write the following:

"Dreams are notoriously elusive. In many cases we wake up fresh from a dream only to find that it is already fading in our memory. Even our more graphic and memorable dreams will fade quickly unless we write them down and have some plan in place for deliberate reflection. This is why a dream book or journal is so useful. It gives you a chance to record your dream, or at least its highlights, while the impressions are still fresh on your mind. Having a definite plan in place for dream reflection and analysis will make you more likely to follow through and take time to think about your dreams.... That is why we need to learn to recognize and overcome dream snatchers, dream *drainers* and dream *busters."*

I love this paragraph because the enemy attempts to interrupt us in the middle of gaining revelation. Most of us are unaware of how he does this during our "night." We seem to be more alert during the day. James and Michal Ann give us some very key practical points on how to overcome the enemy even while we sleep.

In *When God Speaks,* Rebecca Wagner Sytsema and I share the following:

In the Bible, prophecy and dreams were to be tested in the same way and, according to Numbers 12:6, we find that prophecy and dreams were treated equally. Saul complained that God would not speak to him or answer him "by dreams or by Urim or by the prophets" (1 Sam. 28:6). By this we can infer that these were normal ways that people heard from God. We find three types of dreams in the Bible:

1. **A simple message dream.** In Matthew 1-2, Joseph understood the dreams concerning Mary and Herod. There was no real need for interpretation. These dreams were direct, to the point and self-interpreted.

2. **The simple symbolic dream.** Dreams can be filled with symbols. Oftentimes the symbolism is clear enough that the dreamer and others can understand it without any complicated interpretation. For instance, when Joseph had his dream in Genesis 37, he fully understood it, as did his brothers, to the point that they wanted to kill him, even though it had symbols of the sun, moon and stars.

3. **The complex symbolic dream.** This type of dream needs interpretative skill from someone who has unusual ability in the gift of interpretation or someone who knows how to seek God to find revelation. We find this type of dream in the life of Joseph in prison, when he interprets Pharaoh's dream. In Daniel 2 and 4, we find good examples of this type of dream. In Daniel 8, we see a dream where Daniel actually sought divine interpretation.

We are entering a season where the Lord is "reordering our day." If you will remember, the day actually begins at sunset. The Holy Spirit is now restoring the power of the night watch in the Church. We will be arising and praying as well as sleeping and receiving! We must be a trained army of intercessors and leaders who know how to deal very skillfully with the revelation that we receive from the Lord. If we are going to walk in the day and possess our inheritance, we must learn how to rule in the night. Most of our dreams come during the night. I believe James and Michal Ann have created a tool that will be used from one generation to another generation as each wield the sword of revelation to build the Church for the future and unlock the Kingdom of God. *Dream Language* is an excellent source of experiential and practical principles that will assist you in learning to rule the night.

Chuck D. Pierce, President
Glory of Zion International, Inc.
Vice President, Global Harvest Ministries

PART ONE

BUILDING THE FRAMEWORK

M ost of us find ourselves slithering down the stream of chaotic activity, never allowing ourselves to find the shore of silence where we can pause to ponder the mysteries of God's design for our life. Yet, it is in those private places that God's presence and God's word seeks to invade our lives. It is there that the Master Dream Weaver comes to us, eager to reveal Himself in unique and unusual ways.

Through dreams God communicates with us concerning our destiny, as well as the destinies of our families, our nation, and our world. Part One of this book will help you build the framework that will enable you to understand the work of this Weaver in your dream life.

You will also discover that dreams and the interpretation of dreams is neither a modern phenomenon nor a unique event in the life of the God's people. Spiritual dreams have their roots in ancient Judaism, as well as in the early Church. In fact, dreams have been the source of some of the greatest paradigm shifts in the history of Judaism and the Church. Consider Abraham and Peter: The birth of Israel was spoken of as Abraham slept on the desert sands, and Peter's dream opened the door of the Church to the Gentile world!

Because dreams are notoriously elusive, it is important that we have some tools in our hands that will help us capture our dreams for the purpose of interpreting those dreams. After all, what good is a spiritual dream if it is not remembered nor interpreted correctly? Sadly, we would run the risk of losing God's word for our lives.

This first section will provide those simple, yet oft considered mysterious, tools so that you too will become a dream catcher. May all your dreams come true!

CHAPTER ONE

THE MASTER DREAM WEAVER

Have you ever watched a master weaver at work? The speed and fluency of practiced hands flying across the loom and spindle interlacing the strands of fine linen is truly impressive to behold. To the untrained observer there is something almost magical at the sight of warp and weft coming together in perfect harmony to give shape to patterns and designs seen only in the mind's eye of the weaver.

Weaving is one of the oldest of the human arts. Mankind has been weaving fabric for clothing and other purposes since before the dawn of recorded history. Yet for all of its beauty and intricacy, the human art of weaving, like all of man's other creative arts, is but a dim reflection of the creativity and artistry of the Master Weaver Himself, who wove the heavens and the earth together and who created man in His own image.

The psalmist proclaims: *"The heavens are telling of the glory of God; and their expanse is declaring **the work of His hands**"[1]; "When I consider Your heavens, **the work of Your fingers**, the moon and the stars, which You have ordained; what is man that You take thought of him, and the son of man that You care for him?"[2]; "For You formed my inward parts; **You wove me in my mother's womb**. I will give thanks to You, for I am fearfully and wonderfully made; wonderful are Your works, and my soul knows it very well."[3]*

God is a Master Artist and Craftsman, not only of that which is seen but also that which is unseen. He is a Creator by nature and as such is always creating. As the Master Weaver, God is weaving the renowned tapestry of human history; He is interlacing the warp and weft of each of our individual lives into the pattern of His own design. Much of the pattern of this great tapestry consists of the dreams that are such a significant part of each of our lives. This includes not only the hopes and dreams we have for our future but also the dreams that come to us when we are in our state of sleeping.

After all, God is the Master Dream Weaver. Through dreams God communicates directly with us concerning our destiny as well as the destinies of our families, our nation, and our world. Many people today, particularly in the Western culture, never recognize God speaking to them in this way because they have been conditioned by a skeptical and sophisticated society to discount the language of dreams. Unfortunately, this includes many Christian believers also. For many years much of the church in the West had virtually lost dream language as a viable language of the Spirit. Yet, within our own generation the tide has begun to turn. God is reawakening His people to the efficacy of dreams in their lives. He is reconnecting us to a vital part of our spiritual heritage that had all but disappeared.

Sometimes when you look back on a dream you may wonder whether it has any meaning, and if so, what that meaning may be. Is it merely a product of your active subconscious mind with no particular connection to your daily life? Is it a personal dream with a meaning for you alone? Or does it have a wider significance, involving your family, coworker, your city, your nation, or even beyond? You may ponder those images and think, "I don't quite get the picture yet." If you have ever felt this way, don't worry. I too have been daunted by such thoughts over the years. Just keep searching and watch as these mysteries unfold before your very eyes. God wants you to understand your dreams and how they influence your life. He wants to restore your ability to communicate on this spiritual plane. God wants to make you fluent once again in dream language, *the mystical language of Heaven.*

The Mystical Language of Heaven

Simply stated, a dream is a series of thoughts, images, or emotions that appear in our minds during sleep. Sometimes they are straightforward, but most of the time they are not. In the case of Holy Spirit-inspired dreams, often there is the need for careful interpretation, as these dreams tend to be parabolic in nature. In other words, like the parables of Jesus, the meaning of a dream is sometimes hidden.

> *As soon as He was alone, His followers, along with the twelve, began asking Him about the parables. And He was saying to them, "To you has been given the mystery of the kingdom of God, but those who are outside get everything in parables, so that while seeing, they may see and not perceive, and while hearing, they may hear and not understand, otherwise they might return and be forgiven."*[4]

Just as He went off alone with His disciples in that day, Jesus wants to get alone with us as His disciples today. He has special words to release to each of us. In a way, Jesus' words here are strange and even troubling. He indicates that He speaks in parables so those who listen may "see and not perceive" and "hear and not understand." Doesn't the Lord want everyone to seek Him and come to the knowledge of the truth? Of course He does! But His pattern of teaching in His earthly ministry was to speak in parables and mysteries—not to keep people in the dark, but to whet the appetite of those who were truly hungry for the truth. He wanted to lure them in so they would press forward to know more. God likes playing hide and seek. We get to seek out the treasure He has hidden for us! He loves this journey of hooking us with revelation with the purpose of actually reeling us into His very heart.

Even though that Scripture passage does not mention dreams or visions, I have used it here because dreams and visions often use parabolic language and, like parables, are mysteries that need careful deciphering. Dream language is the mystical language of Heaven. And even though it is a language of mystery and parable, we need to understand that God likes to reveal rather than conceal. Just a few verses later Jesus says:

> *"For nothing is hidden, except to be revealed; nor has anything been secret, but that it would come to light. If anyone has ears to hear, let him hear." And He was saying to them, "Take care what you listen to. By your standard of measure it will be measured to you; and more will be given you besides. For whoever has, to him more shall be given; and whoever does not have, even what he has shall be taken away from him."*[5]

The Lord speaks mysteries, secrets, whose meaning is hidden except to those who have a heart and soul to search it out. These scriptural truths give evidence that things are hidden for a divine purpose: the purpose of being revealed. This is very important where dreams and visions are concerned. As you start to study these revelatory ways, be prepared for God to visit you and speak secrets to you—things that in the beginning you might not understand fully. As your journey continues, however, and as you receive more of the spirit of wisdom and revelation, you will gain a much greater understanding of the mysteries and secrets related to heavenly dreams and visions.

Part of the secret is cultivating the skill of listening. Jesus said, "If anyone has ears to hear, let him hear" and "Take care what you listen to." Understanding dream language requires one to be "all ears," in other words, to be attentive. Listening has become a lost art in many ways, but it is a vital skill for any one who desires to become fluent in dream language.

Dreams are indeed the supernatural communication of Heaven— love letters filled with mysteries, intrigue, and divine parables. Dream language is truly a language of the ages. Recorded throughout the Bible, dreams and visions begin in Genesis and run all the way through to the last book of Revelation. Dream language is an accurate and detailed communications tool thoroughly grounded throughout Scripture.

Grounded in the Old Testament

God is a supernatural God who communicates with His people through supernatural means. For example, the Bible refers to angels over 300 times. The words "dream" or "vision" and their variations occur over 200 times. The Bible is full of supernatural encounters. When we talk about the strategic value of dream language, it is important that we be thoroughly grounded in the Word of God while being led by the Holy Spirit at the same time.

It is like learning to operate a sailboat. There are times when you put up the sail to catch the wind so it can drive you along from one point to the next. (The wind represents the moving of the Holy Spirit who guides us and provides us with power for the journey.) At other times we need to enter the harbor, drop the anchor, and be at rest. (The anchor symbolizes the Word of God. We need to take time to study and meditate on

God's Word to renew our minds and refuel our spirits.) But even when we put up the sail and leave the harbor, we carry the anchor—the Word of God—with us at all times. It is our grounding, our sure foundation. Even as the Holy Spirit leads us on a faith adventure that carries us outside our safety zone, the anchor of God's Word keeps our feet firmly planted on the Rock that is Jesus Christ Himself.

From the very beginning God brought dreams and visions into play to convey His message to His people. In Old Testament times in particular, dream language was one of His favorite means of communication: *"Hear now My words: If there is a prophet among you, I, the Lord, shall make Myself known to him in a vision. I shall speak with him in a dream."*[6]

This verse is a good illustration of parallelism in Hebrew poetry, restating the same thought with different words. At the same time it reveals a certain degree of differentiation between the purposes of dreams and visions. God says that He will speak to His people in a dream but He will make Himself known in a vision. He uses both of these instruments to draw us into His purposes. Perhaps in their purest ultimate form, visions reveal who God is. Dreams, in turn, tend to be more personal in nature. *Visions reveal God's nature, while dreams often give us direction or reveal some part of God's plan.* This is not a hard and fast distinction but is a general trend to keep in mind.

Dream language is all about a relentless God who passionately pursues His people. He never quits. It says in Job: *"Indeed God speaks once, or twice, yet no one notices it. In a dream, a vision of the night, when sound sleep falls on men, while they slumber in their beds, then He opens the ears of men, and seals their instruction...."*[7] Sometimes we get so engaged in activity and our minds are so preoccupied that it is hard for us to hear God—but God's love always prevails. If He cannot catch our attention during our waking hours, He will covertly speak to us during our sleep through dreams. Dream language is a love language. Our dreams are love letters sent to us from Papa God. When our guard is down and our analytical skepticism is less active, God whispers in our ear.

Our heavenly Father wants us to start and finish well and He will even use dreams and visions as an avenue of identifying the hindrances that are in our path to His purpose. He will secure cleansing, healing, and deliverance, even in the night seasons. Yes, I speak from personal experience. He has often appeared to me in this language form to release comfort, healing, and empowerment for my walk with Him.

Another foundational Old Testament Scripture regarding dreams and visions is found in the Book of Joel: "*It will come about after this that I will pour out My Spirit on all mankind; and your sons and daughters will prophesy, your old men will dream dreams, your young men will see visions. Even on the male and female servants I will pour out My Spirit in those days.*"[8] The promise of these verses has already been partially fulfilled but not yet to its greatest capacity. A day is coming when the outpouring of God's presence on the earth will be more profuse than at any time since the first century. A great revival will come and the glory of the Lord will cover the earth as the waters cover the seas. Dreams and visions are a major part of the prophetic outpouring of God's great love in the Last Days!

The ultimate purpose of this outpouring of the Spirit of God will be to awaken non-believers. These verses do not state that God will pour His Spirit out only on *believers*—the community of the redeemed in Christ Jesus—but on *all flesh*, and this happens by the Spirit of revelation. God wants His people to be a people of revelation who move in the inner hearing and knowledge of heavenly language of dreams and visions.

Three very similar Hebrew words are used in the Old Testament to refer to dreams. The first of these is *chalam*, which means "to cause to dream" or "to be a dreamer." Second is *chelem*, which simply means "to dream." Finally, there is *chalom*, which denotes "dreamer." Whichever word is used, the Old Testament makes clear that God is the Master Dreamer. He downloads His dreams within us and thereby transforms us into dreamers as well.

Grounded in the New Testament

The New Testament offers us a few more specifics, using two distinct words for "dream": *onar* and *enupnion*. As I noted in my earlier book, *The Seer*:

In Greek, *onar* is the common word for "dream." It refers simply to the kind of dreaming we all do when we sleep. Everyday dreams are themselves visionary in nature because our minds generate images that we "see" while we are asleep. As the Bible makes clear, God can and does use these common dreams to communicate with ordinary people.[9]

Examples of *onar* include Joseph's dreams in the first and second chapters of Matthew regarding his marriage to Mary, their flight to Egypt with the young Jesus to escape Herod's murderous rage, and their return home after Herod's death. On these occasions, even though Joseph experienced dreams during normal sleep, he recognized them as being from the Lord and was quick to obey. The dream of the wise men in which they are warned not to return to Herod is another example of the use of *onar*.

The second New Testament word for "dream" is *enupnion*. Here is a brief explanation of that term:

Like *onar*, the word *enupnion* refers to a vision or a dream received while asleep. The difference with *enupnion* is that it stresses a surprise quality that is contained in that dream.[10]

One example of *enupnion* is found in the Book of Acts when Peter quotes Joel 2:28-29:

"And it shall be in the last days," God says, "that I will pour forth of My Spirit on all mankind; and your sons and your daughters shall prophesy, and your young men shall see visions, and your old men shall dream [enupnion] *dreams."*[11]

Enupnion refers to the kind of dream that has a startling effect. As penned in *The Seer*:

Literally, the phrase "shall dream dreams" means "shall be given up to dream by dreams." This is the kind of dream that really sticks with you after you wake up. Something about it startled you and made your senses alert, perhaps some kind of shocking quality to the dream that causes you to remember it vividly.[12]

Have you ever awakened suddenly from a dream and found yourself strangely alert? Maybe all your senses were particularly acute. The experience may be positive or negative. You may sense an otherworldly presence in the room. This is the kind of dream that the word *enupnion* describes.

We Are the Dream Receivers

If God is the "The Master Dream Weaver" and the "Dream Giver" then we are His "Dream Receivers." The secret to becoming a good dreamer is to become a good receiver. By the grace of God, the heavenly dove not only has spoken in ages past, it speaks today and will express God's thoughts personally to *you* in the future. Before you go to sleep, toss up a simple prayer. Just declare, "Here I am, Lord; I am ready to receive." He will come; He will invade your space. Just receive!

Dreams to Unbelievers

Dreams from God are not limited to committed believers. In fact, the largest category of dreams in the Scriptures is targeted to unbelievers. Here are just a few examples:

1. Abimelech (Gen. 20:3)

2. Laban (Gen. 31:24)

3. Pharaoh's butler and baker (Gen. 40:5)

4. Pharaoh (Gen. 41:1,5)

5. Midian (Judg. 7:13-14)

6. Nebuchadnezzar (Dan. 2:1,4,36)

In the New Testament we also find examples of dreams given to unbelievers, such as the wise men and Pilate's wife (see Matt. 2:12; 27:19).

Why does God send dreams to unbelievers? Because He wants to turn their hearts toward Him! God is unwilling that anyone should perish. He wants all people to "be saved and to come to the knowledge of the truth."[13]

Dreams to Believers

The Bible is also full of references to dreams given to believers—to prophets and other people of God. Abraham, whom God calls a prophet, fell into a deep sleep and "terror and great darkness" suddenly came upon him (Gen. 15:12). In a dream God spoke to him concerning the four centuries of slavery in Egypt that his descendants would endure as well as their deliverance that would follow.[14]

Jacob, Abraham's grandson, received a powerful dream from God that changed the course of his life. Fleeing from the wrath of his brother Esau, Jacob beds down for the night in a wilderness area, using a rock as a pillow for his head. During the night he dreams of a ladder reaching from Heaven to earth with angels ascending and descending. At the top of the ladder Jacob beholds God in all His glory. God promises to accompany Jacob on his journey, to prosper him, and eventually to safely guide him back home.

Upon awakening, Jacob is awestruck by his encounter with God. He takes the stone he utilized as a pillow and positions it as a pillar of remembrance of the day he met the Lord, pouring oil on it as an act of worship.[15] This rock symbolizes Jesus Christ Himself, who is the Rock, the Cornerstone. One of the great truths revealed in this account is the approachability of God. He is not out of touch or beyond reach. He cares about what transpires in our lives and has made Himself available to each of us.

Daniel was another unforgettable dream receiver. The seventh chapter of the Book of Daniel records the prophet's dream of four great beasts, representing four powerful kingdoms that would arise on the earth. The fourth beast, more terrible than any of the others, is destroyed by the Son of Man, who eventually establishes an eternal kingdom.

Genesis 37:1-11 relates Joseph's dreams of how his father and brothers would one day bow down to him. Twenty years later Joseph's dreams were literally fulfilled when, having risen from slave to prime minister of Egypt, he greets his brothers when they come to purchase food as a result of the great famine. More than just a dreamer, Joseph became a dream interpreter. While in prison he interpreted the dreams of Pharaoh's butler and baker, which led in time to his interpreting Pharaoh's dreams concerning the great famine that was imminent. As a result, Pharaoh promoted Joseph to prime minister and put him in charge of storing up food against the famine years.

Solomon, the wisest person who ever lived, received his impartation of wisdom from Jehovah in a dream.[16] God told Solomon to ask for whatever he wished. How amazing is that! Solomon beseeched the Lord for wisdom that he might rule his people well. Pleased with the king's unselfish request, God provided Solomon with wisdom—and more. He also granted him riches and honor greater than any who preceded him and any who would ensue.

Solomon's experience exhibits how dreams from God sometimes have an interactive quality. God sometimes interacts with us through dreams. This proposes not only that He speaks to us, but also that He expects a response from us. Sometimes He releases spiritual empowerment or gift impartation. Sometimes, as with Solomon, God asks a question or elicits a response—not because He does not know the answer, rather, God's questions are ultimately invitations to greater intimacy with Him!

The New Testament also gives some examples of dreams given to believers. Joseph, husband of Mary, had a dream to prepare him for his role of protector and caregiver with wisdom. Then there is Paul, whose dream of a Macedonian man calling for help leads to the introduction of the gospel of Christ into the continent of Europe.[17]

Dream Transmitters

We are dream receivers, and every receiver needs a transmitter. In human experience dream transmission originates from any one of three different sources. The first of these sources is God Himself. God is a personal God who transmits dreams to individuals. These, of course, are spiritual dreams inspired by the Holy Spirit. All of the biblical dreams I have cited so far in this initial chapter are of this type, whether they were received by believers or by unbelievers. Each had their source in God who transmitted the dreams to specific people for His own personal purposes.

It is particularly important to acknowledge God as a primary source of dreams, as we live in a culture where many people either dismiss dreams as irrelevant in the modern age or dismiss the quaint notion that God still speaks today or both. People who take dreams seriously are assumed to be "New Agers" or at least regarded as somewhat weird or even "spooky." Even within the Church many modern believers are suspicious of dreams as being too far out or too "mystical."

However, God is unchanging. He has always been the Master Dream Weaver. He has always employed dreams and visions as one of His primary means of speaking to His people. Dream language is just as viable a vehicle for divine communication today as it has ever been. It is high time for the people of God to reclaim dream language from the "New Agers" and the occultists and restore it once more to its significant place as one of God's modes of speech.

The second transmitter or source of dreams is natural man. Natural or "soulish" dreams and visions are produced by the natural processes of our mind, will, and emotions. Dreaming is a normal part of human brain function when in a deep sleep state. Sights, sounds, smells, and other sensory stimuli from the day provide the raw materials from which our brains create natural dreams. Sometimes, if we are not careful, we can confuse a natural dream with a dream from God. This is especially dangerous when the dream is presented to others as being of divine origin. Scripture cautions us against making such a mistake: *"Thus says the Lord of hosts, 'Do not listen to the words of the prophets who are prophesying to you. They are leading you into futility; they speak a vision of their own imagination, not from the mouth of the Lord.'"* [18]

There is also a third source of dream transmission, originating in the realm of demonic darkness. False and occultic dreams fall into this category. These are dreams that are demonically inspired, deceitfully crafted by evil agents. One biblical example of false revelation is found in Acts 16:16-18 where Paul casts out a python spirit of divination from a slave girl; with this spirit she had brought her masters much profit through fortune telling. The slave girl's "stuff" obviously came from a false source.

It is important, therefore, that we develop and exercise discernment in properly identifying the sources of our various dreams. Dream Language, however, is not something to fear. It is something to cherish!

Purpose and Invitation

Why does God sometimes speak in dream language? What is His purpose? A verse in the Book of Proverbs gives us a clue: "It is the glory of God to conceal a matter, but the glory of kings is to search out a matter." [19] God often uses dreams to reveal by concealing. He wants to stir within us our natural inclination to search out answers. In other words, God has given us an open invitation into kingship.

I believe that seeking to understand dreams is part of the impact of the Reformation of the Church that originated in the 1400–1700s. The Great Reformation restored to the Church the concept of the priesthood of every believer, the power and authority of every believer to relate to

God directly without going through a priest or any other designated authority figure. Jesus Christ is our only Mediator. Through Him we are all ministers and we all have equal access to God the Father.

Yet there is another dimension to this. The Old Testament identified the three basic offices: prophet, priest, and king. In Christ we are all three. We are each priests who petition and prophets who receive. Receiving and understanding dream language in turn moves us into the realm of kings whose glory is to search out a matter. As citizens of the Kingdom we have the right to enter His palace and search out the King of Kings' secrets. He wants to give us the keys of revelation so that we can unlock the meanings behind our dreams. It is the glory of a king to search out a matter! Be a king, and go search it out! This is your inheritance!

This is not a slave mind-set. Slaves have no rights and no access to the King. Understanding revelation is all about being a son or a daughter. It is about kingship. It is about approachability and access to the throne.

As you begin to move in the realm of dream language, God will begin to unfold mysteries for you. He will give you insights to share with others, insights about your city or your family. He will give you things to pray about to block the way of the demonic entrance. What is God's purpose in using dream language? He wants to not only spur us on to search for His message but also put us in intimate touch with the Messenger—Himself. That is His purpose—and His invitation.

God has an awesome plan for your life and He wants to use dream language to speak to *you*. He wants to place the spirit of revelation upon your life and use you to bless and build up other believers. God wants to reveal Himself, His purposes, and His ways.

Our goal as believers is to live in Christ and to release the fragrance of His presence wherever we go. I don't want to live an ordinary life and I am sure you don't either. I want to live a life in the supernatural to such an incredible degree that will cause people to say, "Behold! There is a dreamer."

Is this your desire also? If so, then come along with me. Let's pursue the Master Dream Weaver and His revelatory ways together!

Reflection Questions

1. Jesus spoke in parables. How does this relate to dream language?

2. State an example of dreams given to believers and to unbelievers alike as recorded in the Bible.

3. Do you expect God to speak to you in the realm of dreams? Has He spoken to you in this manner in the past? If so, recite an example.

Referral Readings

Bruce Wilkinson, *The Dream Giver* (Sisters, OR: Multnomah Publishers, Inc., 2003).

Jim W. Goll, *The Seer* (Shippensburg, PA: Destiny Image Publishers, 2004).

CHAPTER TWO

MY PERSONAL
DREAM JOURNEY

People who walk in supernatural "God encounters" often tell how their journey began with bright lights and angels or other wild manifestations of God's power. It was different with me. My personal dream journey had some dark beginnings. I was very young when I first started having supernatural dreams, and they were usually dark in source, content, and even color.

I'll give you a secret tip right here from the beginning. One of the keys to interpreting dreams is to consider the quality of the colors that appear in them. Dreams characterized by dark, subdued, or muted colors typically do not originate from the Holy Spirit. More often the Holy Spirit sends dreams that are full of lively, bright, vivid colors. After all, God is alive and vibrant! The Bible speaks of a rainbow surrounding His throne and an emerald sea before Him. God is full of color! His is a kingdom of *light!* The kingdom of the enemy, however, is full of darkness. Satan's kingdom is a dark kingdom characterized by darkness of mind, spirit, and behavior.

As a child I had one recurring dream in which everything was very gray and dark. A man would appear in the shadows at the foot of my bed and begin taunting me. Then the being would raise a large butcher knife over me. Just as he was ready to plunge the knife down into my body, I would wake up in fear and trembling. As if this gruesome image was not frightening enough for me as a young boy, I remember even more strongly the overall atmosphere of absolute terror that permeated the dream experience. This presence was so strong that even after I woke up in my bedroom in my parents' home in rural Missouri the sensations of terror haunted me.

It would be easy to write off a dream like this as a simple childhood nightmare. But with dreams, often there is more to them than meets the eye. Discernment is critical in this matter. I do believe in praying with parents and their children to silence their nightmares; I have successfully done so with many. At the same time, it is important to understand that even nightmares can signify, if interpreted correctly, a forerunner under-standing of what God wants to do in the life of this child. Quite often, the recurrence of such a dream, even when dark, is an indication of God's call of a spirit of revelation on that child. The enemy may try to shove his way in to distort that call by filling the child's or even adult's mind with dark and dire images of his own design. Always remember, the enemy is only threatened by what challenges him!

In my recurring nightmare, the downward plunge of that butcher knife sometimes catapulted me into an open vision. At the time, of course, I did not even know or understand what an open vision was, let alone how to interpret such events. This did not come till much later!

As I eventually learned, the motivating force behind this activity was actually a spirit of death. The year before I was born, my mother was expecting a little baby boy, but suffered a miscarriage. That day, in her pain and sorrow, she prayed to God and said, "Lord, if You will give me another son, I will dedicate him to Christ's service." I was born exactly one year later, to the very date. However, when I was in the process of being born, the umbilical cord was wrapped around my neck cutting off my breath. Although that is not a highly unusual occurrence in itself, in my case it was a sign of spiritual warfare as the enemy sought even then to literally choke me off from the call that was on my life. Warfare seemed to surround my conception, my birth, and later my childhood; but perhaps there is another side to this as the enemy perceived in part that I had a call to the prophetic and to spiritual warfare. Remember, he is only threatened by what challenges him.

On the positive side, the wrapped umbilical cord caused my head to turn blue; and often, in prophetic circles, blue is symbolically interpreted as the color of revelation. What the enemy meant for evil, God turned around for good. If you are like me and feel you have had a bad or a difficult beginning, I have *good news* for you. God can turn the devil's plans upside down! What satan intended as a curse on your life can be changed into a blessing instead! Remember, God always holds the winning hand!

Early Prayers that Shaped My Life

Thanks in part to my parents, to my upbringing in Sunday School and church, and mainly to God's hand on my life, I developed a deep love for Jesus early in life. As a child I began praying three specific prayers that I continue to pray regularly today. The first of these prayers is, "God, I ask that You would raise up Your Joseph counselors to those in authority like You did in days gone by." Can you imagine a *little kid* praying a prayer like that? It had to be supernaturally inspired. I could never come up with such a prayer on my own!

In my college years and later I became a behind-the-scenes personal intercessor for a man who was first a U.S. senator from Missouri, then the governor, and eventually the Attorney General of the United States: John Ashcroft. The Lord used to show me in dreams and visions how the hand of God rested upon this righteous man and how he would have the spirit of Joseph upon his life. God called me as a young man to pray that John Ashcroft would be raised with the spirit of wisdom as a Joseph counselor to those in authority. And sure enough, it came to pass as John Ashcroft became the Attorney General of the United States. As God leads, I continue to pray in my secret place for the Lord to raise up other "Josephs" who will give counsel to those in authority.

My second prayer in my youth was for wisdom. I prayed, "Lord, like Solomon, give me wisdom beyond my years." The older I get the more I realize how much I still need God's wisdom. Natural training and knowledge are not enough for any of us. To be effective in reaching the world with the gospel of the Kingdom, we need the wisdom of God to enhance our natural abilities, training, and knowledge to take us beyond where we could ever go by ourselves.

My third prayer is inspired by the Beatitudes in the fifth chapter of Matthew: "God, give me a heart of purity that will keep me from the evil way." Purity has always been an important issue for Christians and never more so than today. The temptations to abandon purity have never been stronger or more numerous than in our materialistic, pleasure-driven culture. Through the years I've discovered that these are three of the keys to unlocking the spirit of revelation upon your life or anyone else's. What God did in the past He will do again. Pray for the spirit of counsel, the spirit of wisdom, and a heart of purity.

The "Jesus People" Influence

In 1972, while I was in college, I attended one of the early "Jesus People" gatherings held at the Cotton Bowl in Dallas, Texas. This enormous gathering was hosted by Dr. Bill Bright of Campus Crusade for Christ. Evangelist Billy Graham spoke on the last night and absolutely scorched my life for Jesus Christ. Even today I still have portions of his message on "commitment" seared on my heart. As a result of his message, I dedicated my life to full-time Christian service. Jesus is all I have ever known. He's ultimately all I ever want.

A little over a year ago, a lady drove up several hours from Alabama to our ministry center in Franklin, Tennessee, just to give me a gift: a shirt that she had picked up at a garage sale in southern California. She didn't really understand why, but simply felt led to give the shirt to me. She, of course, did not know any of my personal history. It was a yellow summer shirt that had been worn and owned by Dr. Bill Bright. It even had his name printed in the collar. Campus Crusade for Christ is the largest student campus ministry in the history of Christianity. I did not know for some time what to do with this gift. I actually only put the shirt on once—I slept in it.

Yes, there are dreams, visions, and also prophetic acts. Perhaps that shirt from this prestigious man of God represents a mantle of God's heart for another student movement to come forth that will eclipse anything that has gone before. Perhaps God has a dream in His heart: for millions of young people to come to Christ and spread His Kingdom wherever they go! I have since passed that shirt on to two sold-out young men who are now leaders of a vibrant campus ministry in Nashville, Tennessee, where we live. And the beat goes on.

After the Cotton Bowl event in 1972, I found myself hanging with the Jesus People a lot. Basically, they were hippies who had found Jesus.

They looked and dressed differently than I did but they were so on fire for God! They witnessed to me about things like speaking in tongues, deliverance, and the baptism in the Holy Spirit. Having been raised a Methodist I didn't really understand what they were talking about, but I deeply admired their fervency.

I was willing to accept the idea that God gave those strange things to those who needed them, but *I* did not need them. Eventually, however, the Holy Spirit twisted my arm hard enough to get me to the knowledge that I needed anything He had! And so I became filled with the Holy Spirit with the release of His gifts, including praying and worshiping in the gift of tongues and visions. These gifts became an absolute lifeline for my personal life and eventually my ministry.

Up to that time, I tended to relate to God on what seemed like a little black-and-white TV set. But after being saturated the Holy Spirit, revelation permeated my being and things switched to "omni-vision" overnight. Now I was receiving detailed dreams and visions in full, vivid color. I would walk on the college campus and see a person in the natural whom I had seen in my dream or vision the day or week before—a person I didn't even know. Nevertheless, I started approaching these people and sharing with them what God had shown me. Somehow, it worked. Wow, did it work! And it has never stopped.

Immersed in the Spirit

Once I became immersed in the Spirit, my life began to change in significant and drastic ways. I literally began to have dreams in which I was standing before thousands preaching the gospel. At the time, the thought of getting up in front of even three people scared me, much less to stand before thousands! So that dream, at least, seemed far-fetched. After all, I was a math and science guy. My sights were set on working for NASA as a biologist in research and development. God radically shifted my paradigm though. He totally upended my life goals. He called me to share His love, and later to share, teach, and preach the Good News. He gave me a heart to reach the nations for Christ. And now I could not dream of doing anything else. If you are eager to walk in the deeper things of the Spirit, prepare yourself! He will take your life in directions you have never dreamed.

Never doubt the word or the promise that the Lord gives you in a dream, even if its fulfillment seems long in coming. Recently I was in Bogotá, Colombia, where I had the privilege of preaching to the third-largest church in the world. As I stood in that coliseum where tens of thousands of people were looking back at me, I suddenly felt so inadequate! Panic began to rise in me, and I prayed desperately, "Lord, get me out of here! Do something! I'm not a crusade preacher!"

Suddenly, the Holy Spirit began reminding me of some of my past dreams and things He had spoken to me previously. I experienced a sudden mental paradigm shift and started to see things differently. It was the same coliseum and the same people; yet I had changed. I looked at the crowd around me and said, "Oh, this is just another house. The father of this house has invited me here. I am in another living room, larger than any other I have ever seen, but still a living room." This mental shift occurred just before I was supposed to get up and release my exhortation. When I did, the Holy Spirit empowered me and He really scorched the place! When I got up to that podium, I knew I was born for this! Dreams had imparted courage to me for my assignment.

Yes, dreams and visions are amazing. They will unlock the purposes of God. They will open up new dimensions of life and change the mundane and make it extraordinary. If God can do it with me, He can surely do it for you!

The Master's Degree

In the late 1980s I was ministering in northern Germany. One night I stayed in the home of an American family who worked with the military. In my earlier years, they had been a part of the campus ministry and church that a friend and I had pastored. During the night I received an amazing calling or destiny dream from the Lord in which a seer prophet named John Paul Jackson stood before me. He is a forerunner in the ministry and language of dreams with a long history of excellent teaching on the subject. In my dream his image was two or three times bigger than life-size. He pointed his prophetic finger at me and said, "You will receive the Master's Degree as a communication specialist and an interpreter of speech." I was stunned!

When I woke up, I felt the riveting presence of God all over me and I was catapulted into an open vision where I saw a man bent over in a field, hoeing. The man in the vision straightened up, looked me right in the eye and said, "You will be the answer to our prayers."

I didn't have a clue of the meaning of my dream and vision, especially that vision. Even though I was in Germany, the Goll family's ancestral homeland, I was the first American Goll to return to German soil. At the time, I knew of no righteous generational history.

What did it mean: "You will receive the Master's Degree as a communication specialist and an interpreter of speech"? Later, while traveling through the night in a sleeper car on a train from Heidelberg into Bavaria for six hours, the Holy Spirit kept speaking to me over and over, "Where are the Deborahs? Where are the Josephs? Where are the Esthers? Where are the Daniels?" These questions haunted me until I reached my destination in southern Germany.

The Holy Spirit kept persisting and dealing with me. After the conference was over in Bavaria, I flew from Munich, Germany, to Zagreb to meet my friend Mahesh Chavda where I was to accompany him on miracle crusades in Croatia, which was still part of Yugoslavia at that time. Part of the time I was his personal intercessor and part of the time the daytime minister. From Zagreb we went to Sarajevo, which today is Bosnia-Herzegovina. Then we traveled to Belgrade, Yugoslavia, and on to Prague, Czech Republic. Yugoslavia had just come out from under communism, and the ugly civil war and horrific ethnic cleansing in that region of the world had not begun yet. We were there six months before the unrest broke out. The whole time the Holy Spirit kept saying to me, "Give them all you've got." It was an amazing, truly apostolic moment.

So I gave it everything I had. I took the Spirit's words seriously. At that time my whole approach toward spirit language was to take it all literally. I did not yet understand that dreams usually are more like mysteries or parables rather than literal messages. I pondered on the dream while in Germany and I began to anticipate going back to college for a master's degree in speech communication or some such related field.

When I returned home to Kansas City, I shared my dream and my understanding of it with Mike Bickle and Michael Sullivant. They prayed with me and blessed me for what God was leading me to do. On the one hand I felt that God was requiring me to give up what I'd been doing, to be willing to yield anything and everything to Him. And yet I felt undone—at a loss—all at the same time. After all, had I not answered the call of God to preach the gospel? Now it appeared that the Lord was changing the direction of my life. I investigated different universities for information on their graduate programs to further my quest in becoming a "communications specialist and interpreter of speech."

About the time I had settled in my mind that I had interpreted my dream correctly, the Holy Spirit was about to reveal to me otherwise. I was asked by the leadership of the prominent Kansas City Fellowship to teach on the subject of Prophetic Intercession at one of the big Passion for Jesus conferences. I had never heard anyone teach on the subject, though I had lived in this arena for years. I was definitely leaning hard on the Holy Spirit to be my guide. Four thousand people attended my workshop that day. I looked out at that group and postured myself that this might be my last public hurrah—my last public ministry. You see, I had been up seeking the Lord in the middle of the night in preparation, when I had an angelic visitation with words clearly spoken to me. The Lord's messenger said to me, "Preach as though it's the last time you're ever going to preach."

That afternoon I did just that, and we all had an incredible life-changing encounter with God. I put my whole heart into it. By the end of that day I had taught things I had never been taught and had spoken things I had never previously heard. At the close of the session I asked for the burden of the Lord to be released. I did not teach about travail, but in a sudden swoosh the Spirit of God fell on the room like a blanket and 4,000 people were instantly released into a birthing form of prayer that included moaning, groaning travail. It was an absolutely amazing event! He came! His presence was released in four consecutive overwhelming waves. The burden of the Lord fell en masse and gripped people's hearts.

After it was over I thought for a time, "That's it. What a way to go out! Now I will be going on to something else." Gradually, though, I came to understand that my interpretation of the dream was truly wrong—and if your interpretation is off, your application is doomed! My dream had nothing to do with my going back to a literal graduate school for a literal master's degree, but everything to do with the Master and me. He was saying to me, "I want to give you something that you cannot earn and that you cannot learn in school. I want to give you My Master's Degree."

Yes, it is a journey and a process. Even today I don't know how far along in that journey I have come. I am still in passionate pursuit of the spirit of revelation but also of the grace that was upon Daniel and Joseph, who had the ability to interpret dreams and speak the meaning of mysteries. I have not completed all my courses yet, but I trust that I am further along in my development toward the goal of receiving the "Master's Degree." Why? Because faithful is He who called me (and you) and He will bring it to pass!

Word Grafting

One indispensable aspect of walking wisely and effectively in the realm of dreams and visions is grafting the Word of God into your mind and spirit. James, the apostle to the tribes of Israel in Diaspora, says, "*Therefore, putting aside all filthiness and all that remains of wickedness, in humility receive the word implanted, which is able to save your souls.*"[20] This has been a huge dimension in my own personal walk. Five Scriptures in particular have provided the foundational principles that have guided my personal dream pilgrimage. Let's take a quick glance at each one of them.

> *Therefore Jesus answered and was saying to them, "Truly, truly, I say to you, the Son can do nothing of Himself, unless it is something He sees the Father doing; for whatever the Father does, these things the Son also does in like manner. For the Father loves the Son, and shows Him all things that He Himself is doing; and the Father will show Him greater works than these, so that you will marvel.*"[21]

I grafted these verses into my soul and prayed the principle that even as the Father showed the Son, and the Son could do nothing apart from the Father, so it would be with me. And so it *should* be with all of us. We should ask our Father to show us what He is doing so that we can model it in the earth.

> *And do not go on presenting the members of your body to sin as instruments of unrighteousness; but present yourselves to God as those alive from the dead, and your members as instruments of righteousness to God. For sin shall not be master over you, for you are not under law but under grace. What then? Shall we sin because we are not under law but under grace? May it never be! Do you not know that when you present yourselves to someone as slaves for obedience, you are*

slaves of the one whom you obey, either of sin resulting in death, or of obedience resulting in righteousness?[22]

In other words, if you want to mature in the spirit of revelation, separate all the members of your body unto righteousness. Present every member of your being to be mastered by the Lord Jesus Christ. Surrender! Then graft His Word into your spirit and soul. Let it become, in a sense, *incarnate* in you. Obedience then happens by being empowered by His marvelous grace!

...that the God of our Lord Jesus Christ, the Father of glory, may give to you a spirit of wisdom and of revelation in the knowledge of Him. I pray that the eyes of your heart may be enlightened, so that you will know what is the hope of His calling, what are the riches of the glory of His inheritance in the saints, and what is the surpassing greatness of His power toward us who believe. These are in accordance with the working of the strength of His might....[23]

This third set of verses from Ephesians remains yet today my primary prayer tool and guide. I have probably prayed these verses ten times a day for over ten years, declaring something like, "Open the eyes of my heart, Lord, that I might see You and know Your ways. Send shafts of revelatory light my way in Jesus' name!" In fact, I just went on a walk in the beautiful rolling hills of Franklin, Tennessee, rehearsing once again the power of these words. This is critical for walking successfully in the revelatory realms. Want to know His will and fulfill your destiny? Then pray these and other similar Scriptures over yourself. It will be impossible to live a boring, passive existence.

Then Elisha prayed and said, "O Lord, I pray, open his eyes that he may see." And the Lord opened the servant's eyes and he saw; and behold, the mountain was full of horses and chariots of fire all around Elisha.[24]

I have prayed that, like Elisha's servant, my spiritual eyes would be opened so that I could see into the revelatory realm. In the beginning I was a hearer, not a seer. I could feel but rarely did I see. Dreams were not my first revelatory language. But I kept persisting—and so can you! Pray that the Lord will open your eyes to this realm also.

Then they said to him, "We have had a dream and there is no one to interpret it." Then Joseph said to them, "Do not interpretations belong to God? Tell it to me, please."[25]

This fifth Scripture that I regularly grafted into my soul came from the life of Joseph. Joseph understood that not only did dreams come from the Lord, but their interpretations did also. Don't pray only for dream language. Pray also for the ability to interpret your dreams (and the dreams of others). The same God who gives you the dreams can also enable you to interpret them.

Yes! God answers prayers based on His very Word!

A Wife Who Soars

In the fall of 1992 an enormous change occurred in our family when Michal Ann, my sweet, compliant wife, received a divine visitation that transformed her life—and mine. It was October 4, the Day of Atonement. Michal Ann and I were sound asleep when lightning struck near the back of our house, flashing brightly through our bedroom window. I woke up suddenly and glanced at the clock: 11:59. Immediately, I was intensely aware of a divine presence in the room. A man stood in the bedroom looking at me. I looked back at him. A full minute passed in complete silence: 12:00. Then he said to me, "Watch your wife. I am about to speak to her."

After the angel departed, the sense of divine presence actually increased, and my wife woke up. "Ann," I whispered, "an angel just came." We both pulled the covers over our heads and sat in the bed trembling for over half an hour. Then, somehow, supernaturally, I fell asleep again. Michal Ann was alone with God, and He began rearranging her whole life. Caught up into the spirit realm, she felt as though a board was placed on her back. Pressure was brought to bear, so forcefully that it felt as though the very breath were being pushed out of her. This pressure caused moans and groans to come from deep inside her. This went on for several minutes. As soon as it was over, I woke up again.

This encounter put our lives into a whole new orbit because for the next nine weeks the dreams, visions, and spirit of revelation did not center around me. It was Michal Ann's turn. I was busy traveling and speaking at different places and I would have to phone home to find out what

God was saying. Roles had changed because He was speaking to Michal Ann rather than primarily to me.

Early in my ministry I had barely believed in women in ministry, much less women in leadership. Through the years God had rearranged my thinking on that score. But now God was changing my wife into someone I hardly recognized. Late one night, about halfway through this period, we were standing in our kitchen together. We both were struggling with attention and strange feelings that these changes had produced. I looked at her and said, "I don't know who you are or who you are becoming." She pointed at me with her newly anointed prophetic finger and replied, "Good! I don't know who I am or who I am becoming either!" At that point we realized that we could still walk together because we were still in agreement!

During those nine weeks our lives changed dramatically. I was now married to a wife who soared. She had supernatural visitations almost every night. Why at night? Well, Ann had long yearned for personal intimate encounters with God. However, the pressure of being a stay-at-home mom with four young children, living in a basement in some dear friend's home while our new house was being completed, and my being gone so often on ministry trips was overwhelming at times. One night after I had returned from a weekend trip and related to her God's amazing presence, Ann silently leaned against that basement wall, exhausted and frustrated to the point of tears, and prayed, "Oh God, I just want to be with You. I just want to spend time with You. I just want to hear You."

God spoke comfort into her heart. He said, "I know you don't have much time, but I am going to come to you in the night seasons. I will speak to you in dreams." He began coming immediately, true to His promise, in a targeted manner. These dream experiences were foundation stones being laid in preparation for the coming visitation, which began on the Day of Atonement, 1992. God fulfilled His promise to Michal Ann.

This experience changed our lives forever, but Michal Ann and I have come to believe that God's purpose in all of this reaches far beyond just us. We believe that our experience is also a parable for the Body of Christ. Christ is coming to awaken His Bride. He is going to release dreams and visions, angelic visitations, and signs and wonders, and the ones who have been timid will be changed by His presence.[26]

Guided in the Night

Spiritual dreams are part of our inheritance as children of God. The Father uses them to communicate with us, to reveal His will, to encourage and comfort us, and to inform us of how we should intercede for particular people, situations, and events. Generally, spiritual dreams fall into any one of three basic categories:

1. God speaking to our spirit;

2. Our spirit crying out to God;

3. God's Spirit interceding through our spirit.

I love all three of these dimensions. I love it when God speaks directly to my spirit through a dream. I love it when He awakens me in the night and my spirit cries out to Him. And I love it when His Spirit, in union with mine, intercedes and even enters a spiritual warfare arena through a dream or other God Encounter.

Like Michal Ann, I have had many experiences of being guided by dreams in the night. I have received dreams of a personal nature, dreams about the church, dreams about cities, dreams about nations, dreams about wars, and dreams calling me to intercede so that wars will stop.

One dream that had great significance for me personally occurred in August 2003. I saw a great army coming up to me. Huge in number, the closer they got the more formidable they seemed to me. I began to fear that they were going to overwhelm me completely. Then, suddenly, the whole perspective of my dream changed. I was standing on a horizontal plain, on the same level as they, and as they approached I began to grow, rising up until I was two or three times my normal stature. Now I was looking down on my enemies. That huge army, once so formidable in appearance, now seemed to be nothing more than little stick figures only a few inches tall, lined up in neat little rows.

As I surveyed this changed scene, a word came to me on the wind (often a sign of angelic activity): "And your enemies shall become like grasshoppers in your own sight."

I woke up and thought, "Wow! That will really preach good!" I thought the dream was imparting a message for me to teach others—and it may have been. However, about three weeks later I found a suspicious lump under my skin, which quickly grew to the size of a cluster of grapes. I was diagnosed with non-Hodgkin's Lymphoma cancer.

I thought back to my dream of a few weeks before. Little had *I* "dreamed" at the time that I would be the one who needed the message of that dream! Yet *God* knew. Isn't He such a gracious and merciful and loving Father!

We took my dream and we submitted it to friends and leaders and elders in the city. We submitted it to those we walked with and to our prayer partners. I asked them, "Help me keep my feet to that dream, that my enemies, the enemies of my soul, will become like grasshoppers in my own sight." God is good. He is victorious. We prayed my dream, and I still stand on God's promise today that came to me in that amazing dream. "And your enemies shall become like grasshoppers in your own sight."

I have the same prayer for you, that the Lord will make the enemies of your soul to become like grasshoppers in your own sight! Yes, soon, even satan shall be trampled under the feet of the Body of Christ (see Rom. 16:20).

Dream language is part of our legacy as Christians. Yet there are many in the church today who doubt or deny the efficacy or validity of dreams as a vehicle for divine revelation in the contemporary world. But the Body of Christ has a rich heritage of dream language, beginning with ancient Judaism—in which the Church has its roots—continuing through 2,000 years of revelatory history. To be even more firmly planted in that good soil, let's take a closer look at our legacy in the next chapter.

Reflection Questions

1. What are the three prayers that James prayed as a youth to help cultivate a spirit of revelation? Which one of these could you adapt?

2. There are five sets of Scriptures that James prayed over his life as part of the process of grafting the Word of God into his life. What are two of those references mentioned?

3. There are three basic categories of spiritual dreams. What are they? What category seems to be the primary way that the Lord works with you?

Referral Readings

Benny Thomas, *Exploring the World of Dreams* (Springdale, PA: Whitaker House, 1987).

James W. and Michal Ann Goll, *God Encounters* (Shippensburg, PA: Destiny Image Publishers, 2005).

CHAPTER THREE

DREAM LEGACY
IN HEBRAIC AND
CHRISTIAN HISTORY

Most Christians today are virtually ignorant of the rich heritage of dream language and revelation bequeathed to them by the Church throughout its history. Actually, this legacy is older than the Church. Christian dream language, like the Church itself, has its roots in ancient Judaism. With such a long history, why is this important dimension of Christian experience either unknown or dismissed by so many believers?

Part of the problem lies with the influence of cessationist teaching. Cessationism is the belief that the impartation of spiritual gifts, particularly the sign gifts of prophecy, healing, miracles, and tongues, ceased with the death of the last apostle or when the written canon of Scripture was completed. This teaching holds that the gifts of the Spirit were necessary in the formative days of the Church, but are no longer needed since we now have the completed Bible as our authority, revelation, and guide for Christian living.

Cessationist teaching has done great damage to the Church by discouraging countless believers from pursuing and experiencing the fullest life in the Spirit that they might otherwise enjoy. Scripture itself says that *"Jesus Christ is the same yesterday and today and forever."*[27] With God, there is *"no variation or shifting shadow."*[28] In other words, God never changes. What God did long ago, and throughout history, He does today and will continue always to do. He is eternally the God of *now*. Dream language is the language of the ages. This is one of the mysterious ways that God intersects our lives. He invades our comfort zones. He visits us in the night and simply speaks to us.

Dream language has gotten a bad rap in the church also because of its wide acceptance among "New Agers." Check out the New Age section of any bookstore, and you will find plenty of books on dreaming, dream types and categories, and dream interpretation. Many Christians reason that anything popular with the New Age movement must not have anything to do with the Church. They are right from a certain perspective, of course. But dreaming is *not* the exclusive province of the New Age. In fact, the New Age movement hijacked the concept of spiritual dreams from a much older biblical tradition. It is high time that we, the true Church of Jesus Christ, take back our inheritance and stop giving away our territory to the kingdom of darkness. It's payback time!

Dreams, visions, and interpretations are a part of virtually every culture and religion on earth and have been throughout the ages. This is even truer for Judaism and Christianity than any of the other religions, as Jews and Christians worship the one true God, who is the author of revelation. To accept dreaming as a legitimate medium for spiritual revelation and communication, then, is to follow the flow of history, especially biblical and church history.

Our Hebraic Inheritance

As I mentioned in the first chapter, the concept of dreams and visions as a spiritual means by which God speaks to us is firmly grounded in the Old Testament. Like all the other cultures around them, the ancient Hebrews were very open to dreams as a channel of divine communication. At the same time, however, their approach to dreams was more critical and less superstitious than that of the pagan cultures of their day.[29] This was due in part to their knowledge and understanding of the true God as He had revealed Himself to them. Because dream language was considered a language of the gods, it was prone to falsification and misuse by false prophets and other charlatans who were after their own advantage. For this reason, "the Bible does not express only reverence for dreams; it also offers critical evaluation of them so that people will not be duped by false religions and false religious leaders."[30]

The Hebrew language makes little distinction between a dream and a vision. Although sometimes the two experiences were distinguished from each other, more often the Jews viewed them as merely different aspects of the same basic perception of the supernatural.[31] Indeed, to the ancient Jews, all supernatural communications with God—whether talking directly with Him, receiving angelic visitations, or through dreams, visions, or prophecy—were various expressions of the same basic encounter with a nonphysical reality. And the most common of these by far was the dream experience.[32]

The Old Testament is full of people who had personal divine encounters in this broader sense: Enoch, Noah, Abram (Abraham), Jacob, Joseph, Moses, Joshua, Gideon, Manoah and his wife (Samson's parents), Samuel, David, Solomon, Job, Elijah, Elisha, Isaiah, Jeremiah, Ezekiel, Daniel, Jonah, and the rest of the prophets.

Simply being open to dreams and visions, however, was not enough. The Jews also placed great importance on proper interpretation of dreams and visions and in discerning whether or not they represented the voice of the Lord. This focus on dream analysis was based on Deuteronomy 18:9-22, the only passage in the Law, in fact, that specifically addresses dreams and visions.[33] The passage contains both a prohibition and a promise. The Israelites were told that when they entered and possessed the land of Canaan, they should have nothing to do with the pagan religions of the Canaanites with their witchcraft, sorcery, divination, spells, mediums, omen interpretation, invoking of the dead, and other occultic practices.

God's promise, on the other hand, was: "I *will raise up a prophet from among their* [Israel's] *countrymen like you* [Moses], *and I will put My words in his mouth, and he shall speak to them all that I command him.*"[34] And how will the people know if the prophet has spoken a word of the Lord? "*When a prophet speaks in the name of the Lord, if the thing does not come about or come true, that is the thing which the Lord has not spoken. The prophet has spoken it presumptuously; you shall not be afraid of him.*"[35]

Godly Jews took very seriously every prophetic utterance or other revelatory message, including dreams. While they were quite open, and even expectant, to hearing God speak in this way, they also applied careful standards for analyzing the validity of the message and the messenger; in doing so, they established a precedent that still applies for us today. In our own dream journey we must remember as well the New Testament biblical warning, *"Beloved, do not believe every spirit, but test the spirits to see whether they are from God, because many false prophets have gone out into the world."*[36]

Jewish Dream Practices[37]

Even today observant Jews take divine dreams and dream language very seriously. They even have a well-established tradition of ritual bedtime prayers designed to prepare the heart and mind for sleep and to be open to God's visitation through dreams. Many Jews learn these prayers and principles in an abbreviated form early in childhood as they hear their parents recite them each night. "For both adults and children, this bedtime ritual expresses gratitude for the day that has passed and creates a passageway from the waking state into a meaningful dream life."[38]

Certain dream practices can be added to the traditional prayers to enhance one's spiritual preparation for dreaming. These include the use of a *sefer chalomot,* or "dream book," and a time of *cheshbon hanefesh,* or reflection, where one takes a soul inventory.[39]

Before we can understand our dreams, we must reflect on them; and before we can reflect on them, we must be able to remember them. That is the purpose of the *sefer chalomot.* Keeping a diary or journal by our bedside can aid us in remembering dreams. It makes it easy for us to record our dreams as soon as we wake up, even if it is the middle of the night. Even a folder or binder of blank loose-leaf paper will do—anything that will provide a comfortable format for recording dreams.

Sometimes all it takes to recall your dreams is to make a personal commitment to yourself to remember them. If you are not in the habit of remembering or recording your dreams, be patient. It will probably take a little time to develop this ability.[40]

So here we have three basic principles for handling dream language that have come down to us from Hebrew tradition. First, we expect God to speak. Second, we expect God to enable us to remember what He has given us. Third, we keep a dream book on hand to record our dreams. Isn't that simple?

The second step in Jewish bedtime dream preparation, the *cheshbon hanefesh,* is a reflective activity where we take the time to review our day and take an inventory of our soul. Reviewing our day just before we go to sleep can help center our thoughts and encourage enlightening, productive dreams.[41] This nightly *cheshbon hanefesh* is a smaller version of the self-inspection that Jews do on the days between Rosh Hashanah (the New Year) and Yom Kippur (the Day of Atonement). It is during this time that Jews reflect on their life over the past year and review it analytically before moving into a new year.[42]

If you have never tried a regular self-inspection such as this, you may be wondering how to go about it. Here are some questions to help you get started. As you begin your personal reflection, consider the following:

- What happened today?

- Whom did you encounter?

- What were some of the different feelings you experienced?

- What did you feel proud of?

- What do you wish you could improve upon?

- Whom would you like to forgive? Could you give someone who annoyed you the benefit of the doubt?

- Whom would you wish to apologize to for any mistakes you have made? Whom would you like to ask for forgiveness?

- How would you wish God to forgive you?

- Would you like to pray for someone's health or happiness?

- What are your hopes for tomorrow?[43]

Questions such as these can help put our minds in a reflective state more conducive to receiving dreams. They also help connect our hearts to the heart of our Father and set our minds to look to the Rock, Jesus Christ, from which we are hewn.

Jewish Bedtime Prayers

The *cheshbon hanefesh* prepares the heart and mind for the *tefilah,* the bedtime prayers themselves. These actually constitute one prayer in three parts. "The first part is the *Ha'mapil* ('The One who casts') prayer, in which we ask God for a night of good dreams and the secure feeling of protection as we sleep:"[44]

Blessed are You, our God, gracious One, Keeper of the World,

Who makes my eyes sleepy and causes my eyelids to close.

God of those who came before me,

Help me to lie down peacefully and rise up peacefully.

While I sleep, may I not be disturbed by troubling ideas,

bad dreams, or scary thoughts that come to me in the night.

May my sleep bring both rest and insight.

Blessed are You, God, for illuminating

the whole world in glorious ways.

Part two of the prayer is the familiar *Sh'ma* that is known to many, Jews and non-Jews alike. Taken from Deuteronomy 6:4, the *Sh'ma* is the core statement of Jewish belief and loyalty:

Hear, O Israel, the Lord our God,

the Lord is One.[46]

The Jewish Dream Book goes on to explain:

The third and final part of the bedtime prayer is referred to as the Angels' Prayer, which calls upon God to send God's angels to protect us in the night and enable us to feel the security of their presence. ...On your right side is Michael, the angel of love; on your left is Gabriel, the angel of power; before you is Uriel, the angel of light; behind you is Raphael, the angel of healing; and over you is the *Shekhinah*, God's immanent presence.[47]

This prayer goes as follows:

In the name of the Lord, God of Israel:

May the angel Michael be at my right side,

and at my left side, Gabriel,

before me Uriel,

behind me Raphael,

and above my head, *Shekhinah* El,

God's presence.[48]

There is great wisdom—and centuries of experience—behind these prayers, as simple and even childlike as they may seem. But remember, Jesus said, "Whoever does not receive the kingdom of God as a little child will by no means enter it."[49] Childlike faith is God-pleasing faith, the kind of faith that gives us access to His presence.

This is part of our heritage, something that has been lost to the Body of Christ. It is time for us as followers of Christ to return to our Hebraic roots and expect to receive even in our sleep. Let's make the shift from the Greek practice of over-emphasizing the mind and return to a heart-to-heart, spirit-to-spirit encounter with the living God!

Dream Legacy of the Early Church

Just as they had for the Jews in the Old Testament, divine dreams continued to play a significant role in the New Testament and in the life of the early Church. Matthew, for example, records four dreams that Joseph received relating to the birth and early life of Jesus,[50] as well as the dream to the wise men warning them not to return to Herod.[51] In the Book of Acts, Luke relates Saul's (Paul's) vision of Jesus on the road to Damascus[52] and the subsequent vision of Ananias, whom the Lord sent to lay his hands on Saul and restore his sight. He also mentions Saul's vision in which he is told to expect Ananias.[53] Years later, Paul has a vision that results in his carrying the gospel into the continent of Europe for the first time.[54] Simon Peter and Cornelius, a Roman centurion, both receive visions that lead to Peter's visit to Cornelius's home, where he preaches the gospel to Cornelius and his friends and family.[55]

After the deaths of the apostles and the passing of the New Testament period, church leaders during the first few centuries of the church remained quite open to dreams and visions as a valid avenue of God's communication with man. Many of them wrote of dreams and visions in a positive manner, and some even recorded their personal dream experiences. Polycarp, bishop of Smyrna and a man who was a contemporary of the apostles and was ordained by them, was martyred for his faith in A.D. 155. While praying shortly before his death, Polycarp received a vision in which the pillow under his head caught fire. He understood that this image was a premonition from God of his own impending death.[56]

Justin Martyr, the first Christian philosopher, believed that dreams are sent by spirits. He used this idea to support his belief that the human soul lives on after the death of the body. Dreams give us "direct spiritual communication with nonphysical realities."[57]

Irenaeus, bishop of Lyons in the last half of the second century, believed, like Justin Martyr, that dreams reveal the spiritual world. In *Against Heresies*, his major extant work, Irenaeus provides critical and positive analysis of the dreams of Joseph, Peter, and Paul in the New Testament. He also used his understanding of dreams to refute the idea of reincarnation. Since dreams connect our soul to the spiritual world, we should remember dreams from a former life if such existed.[58]

Clement of Alexandria, one of the most brilliant minds in the early church, believed that true dreams arise from the "depth of the soul" and that they "reveal spiritual reality, the intercourse of the soul with God."[59] For Clement, sleep was a time when a person becomes especially open to divine revelation. Dreams can provide insight to a person's divine destiny:

> Thus also such dreams as are true, in the view of him who reflects rightly, are the thoughts of a sober soul, undistracted for the time by the affections of the body, and counseling with itself in the best manner…. Wherefore always contemplating God, and by perpetual converse with him inoculating the body with wakefulness, it raises man to equality with angelic grace, and from the practice of wakefulness it grasps the eternity of life.[60]

Tertullian, a powerful writer and defender of the faith in the third century, regarded dreams as one of the *charismata*, or spiritual gifts from God. He also believed that they were just as relevant for people of his own day as they were in New Testament days.[61] In his view, dreams came from any one of four sources: demons, God, the soul, or "the ecstatic state and its peculiar conditions."[62]

Augustine, one of the most brilliant minds and greatest theologians in the history of the church, was a firm believer in the validity and value of spiritual dreams. He wrote that humans perceive reality in four different ways. First, there is the outer realm of physical objects to which we react with our physical bodies. Second are the mental impressions that we have of those physical experiences. Third is the inner perception of those experiences; and finally, there is the mental image in its remembered form.[63] Augustine believed that, in addition to physical realities perceived through outer and inner perception, humans could also perceive "autonomous spiritual realities," such as angels and demons, that presented themselves to the inner eye.[64] Augustine's writings contain numerous examples and discussions of dreams, both his own and those of others. One of particular interest is a dream that his mother Monica had received years earlier in which the Lord gave her comfort in the assurance that he (Augustine) would one day turn to Christ.

Thomas Aquinas, a medieval theologian who rivaled Augustine, agreed with Aristotle's view that the only sources of human knowledge are sense experience and rational thought. His approach to theology was to combine Christian thought with Aristotelian thought and thereby to thoroughly modernize Christianity.[65]

Yet, even while writing his massive work, *Summa Theologica,* Aquinas himself experienced both a dream and a revelatory vision. The dream was an instructive dream in which Peter and Paul instructed him on how to handle a particular theological issue he had been having great difficulty with.[66] Near the end of his life, when his great work was almost finished, Aquinas received a vision, a direct divine experience that apparently exceeded anything his rational thought could have produced. The result was that he stopped working on his *Summa Theologica,* saying, "I can do no more. Such things have been revealed to me that all I have written seemed like straw, and I now await the end of my life."[67] And this from a man whose utterly rational approach to theology helped to turn the church as a whole *away* from sensitivity to dream language for centuries!

Dream Language in the Modern Church

By "modern church," I mean the church since the time of the Reformation. Beginning sometime in the fourth century and continuing for over a thousand years, the church officially turned its back on dream language in favor of a more "rational" approach to theology and doctrine. During the same time, however, many individual believers continued to experience dreams and visions of a divine nature, and a large number of the records of those encounters survive to the present day. In other words, despite the church's "official" anti-dream stance, God has continued to speak to His people through dreams and visions just as He did in ancient days. Although there are many examples of this, here we will simply look at two.

John Newton was one of the most respected and loved churchmen in England in the 18th century, but his life did not start off in that direction. Newton grew up, became a seaman, and later became a slave trader. Years later, as he was about to enter the ministry, he wrote about a dream he had had early in his slave-trading days that both warned him of the danger of his way of life and gave him a sense of God's providence. In his dream, Newton was aboard a ship in the harbor of Venice, taking the night watch. A person approached him with a ring, gave it to him, and warned him to guard it carefully because as long as he kept the ring he would be happy and secure.

As he thought about these things, a second person came up to him and convinced him of the folly of depending on the ring for his security. Newton dropped the ring in the water and immediately saw fire burst from a range of mountains behind Venice. Too late he recognized the second person as the tempter, who had tricked him into throwing away God's mercy on his life. All that awaited him now were the hellish flames of those burning mountains. In Newton's own words:

> And when I thought myself upon the point of a constrained departure, and stood, self-condemned, without plea or hope, suddenly a third person, or the same who brought the ring at first, came to me...and demanded the cause of my grief. I told him the plain case, confessing that I had ruined myself willfully, and deserved no pity. He blamed my rashness, and asked if I should be wise supposing I had my ring again.

> I could hardly answer to this; for I thought it was gone beyond recall. Immediately, I saw this unexpected friend go down under the water, just in the spot where I had dropped the ring, and he soon returned, bringing the ring with him. The moment he came on board the flames in the mountains were extinguished, and my seducer left me. My fears were at an end, and with joy and gratitude I approached my kind deliverer to receive the ring again, but he refused to return it, and spoke to this effect:

"If you should be entrusted with this ring again, you would very soon bring yourself into the same distress. You are not able to keep it; but I will preserve it for you, and, whenever it is needful, produce it on your behalf."

After a short time, Newton forgot this dream. A few years later, however, he found himself in circumstances remarkably similar to those in his dream when he "stood helpless and hopeless upon the brink of an awful eternity." There John Newton found mercy from the Lord. He discovered that the One who restored the ring would also keep it for him. This experience led him to exclaim, "O what an unspeakable comfort is this, that I am not in my own keeping!"[68]

As a minister of the gospel, John Newton penned the words to many hymns, including one of the most famous and most often sung hymns of the church, "Amazing Grace." It was a grace that John Newton knew from experience.

The second example is that of the Reverend A. J. Gordon, a Baptist pastor in Boston who became one of the great pulpiteers in America in the 19th century. Reverend Gordon never paid much attention to dreams until the night he had a dream that transformed his entire ministry. His account of his dream, although lengthy, is so compelling that it needs to be shared in its entirety.

It was Saturday night, when wearied from the work of preparing Sunday's sermon, that I fell asleep and the dream came. I was in the pulpit before a full congregation, just ready to begin my sermon, when a stranger entered and passed slowly up the left aisle of the church looking first to the one side and then to the other as though silently asking with his eyes that someone would give him a seat. He had proceeded nearly halfway up the aisle when a gentleman stepped out and offered him a place in his pew, which was quietly accepted. Excepting the face and features of the stranger everything in this scene is distinctly remembered—the number of the pew, the Christian man who offered its hospitality, the exact seat which was occupied. Only the countenance of the visitor could never be recalled.

That his face wore a peculiarly serious look, as of one who had known some great sorrow, is clearly impressed on my mind. His bearing too was exceedingly humble, his dress poor and plain, and from the beginning to the end of the service he gave the most respectful attention to the preacher. Immediately as I began my sermon, my attention became riveted on this hearer. If I would avert my eyes from him for a moment they would instinctively return to him, so that he held my attention rather than I held his till the discourse was ended.

To myself I said constantly, "Who can that stranger be?" And then I mentally resolved to find out by going to him and making his acquaintance as soon as the service should be over. But after the benediction had been given, the departing congregation filed into the aisles and, before I could reach him, the visitor had left the house.

The gentleman with whom he had sat remained behind however; and approaching him with great eagerness I asked: "Can you tell me who that stranger was who sat in your pew this morning?"

In the most matter-of-course way he replied: "Why, do you not know that man? It was Jesus of Nazareth."

With a sense of the keenest disappointment I said: "My dear Sir, why did you let him go without introducing me to him? I was so desirous to speak with him."

And with the same nonchalant air of the gentleman replied: "Oh, do not be troubled. He has been here today, and no doubt he will come again."

And now came an indescribable rush of emotion. As when a strong current is suddenly checked, the stream rolls back upon itself and is choked in its own foam, so the intense curiosity which had been going out toward the mysterious hearer now returned upon the preacher: and the Lord himself "whose I am and whom I serve" had been listening to me today. What was I saying? Was I preaching on some popular theme in order to catch the ear of the public? Well, thank God it was of himself I was speaking. However imperfectly done, it was Christ and him crucified whom I was holding up this morning. But in what spirit did I preach? Was it "Christ crucified preached in the crucified style?" or did the preacher magnify himself while exalting

Christ? That I was about to ask the brother with whom he had sat if the Lord had said anything to him concerning the sermon, but a sense of propriety and self-respect at once checked the suggestion.

Then immediately other questions began with equal vehemence to crowd into the mind. "What did he think of our sanctuary, its Gothic arches, its stained windows, its costly and powerful organ? How was he impressed with the music and the order of the worship?" It too did not seem at that moment as though I could ever again care or have the smallest curiosity as to what men might say of preaching, worship, or church, if I could only know that he had not been displeased, that he would not withhold his feet from coming again because he had been grieved at what he might have seen or heard.

We speak of "a momentous occasion." This, though in sleep, was recognized as such by the dreamer—a lifetime, almost an eternity of interest crowded into a single solemn moment. One present for an hour who could tell me all I have so longed to know; who could point out to me the imperfections of my service; who could reveal to me my real self, to whom, perhaps, I am most a stranger; who could correct the errors in our worship to which long usage and accepted tradition may have rendered us insensible. While I had been preaching for a half-hour he had been here and listening who could've told me all this and infinitely more— and my eyes had been holden that I knew him not; and now he had gone. "Yet a little while I am with you and then I go unto him that sent me."

One thought, however, lingered in my mind [and] was something of comfort and more of awe. *"He has been here today, and no doubt he will come again"*; and mentally repeating these words as one regretfully meditating on a vanished vision, "I awoke, and it was a dream." No, it was not a dream. It was a vision of the deepest reality, a miniature of an actual ministry, verifying the statement often repeated that sometimes we are most awake toward God when we are asleep toward the world.[69]

Reverend Gordon testified that as a result of this dream he never again preached a sermon to please men. Rather, he preached as though his guest was the Man Christ Jesus Himself, and he preached to please Him.

Dreams are powerful things. They can reach us, touch us, and change our lives in a way that no other form of communication can. Don't despise dreams. Don't turn your back on them as so many in the church did for so many centuries. Open yourself to the world of dream language and, in the tradition of the Jews, expect God to speak to you through dreams, expect to remember what He says, and expect your life to be changed as you respond to what God says to you.

Like our Jewish forerunners and the early church fathers, let's create a culture where the spirit of revelation not only exists but flourishes. It's time to take back our spiritual birthright and be sons and daughters who walk an illumined path by the One who is the author of dreams.

Reflection Questions

1. What are some of the primary points concerning Jewish Bed-time Prayers and their possible application for you?

2. Who were some of the early church fathers mentioned in this chapter and their views concerning dreams?

3. Recite the dream of Reverend A.J. Gordon and its meaning for you.

Referral Readings

Morton Kelsey, *God, Dreams, and Revelation* (Minneapolis, MN: Augsburg Press, 1991).

Vanessa L. Ochs, *The Jewish Dream Book* (Woodstock, VT: Jewish Lights Publishing, 2003).

CHAPTER FOUR

CREATING A CULTURE
FOR REVELATION

At this point you may be thinking, "Okay, okay! Dreams are important! God does still speak through dreams and visions. But do I really need a detailed plan for learning to deal with them? Is it really necessary to keep a dream book or journal handy?"

Perhaps not, if you happen to be one of the few who routinely remember your dreams in detail or if you already have developed the mental discipline of pondering and properly analyzing your dreams. If you're like most people, however, you have trouble recalling your dreams except for the occasional vivid nightmare or other powerful dream that leaves a deep impression on your mind.

Dreams are notoriously elusive. In many cases we wake up fresh from a dream only to find that it is already fading in our memory. Even our more graphic and memorable dreams will fade quickly unless we write them down and have some plan in place for deliberate reflection. This is why a dream book or journal is so useful. It gives you a chance to record your dream, or at least its highlights, while the impressions are still fresh on your mind. Having a definite plan in place for dream reflection and analysis will make you more likely to follow through and take time to think about your dreams.

There are many reasons why we seem to lose our dreams even after they have been caught. For one thing, we live in a culture that is so locked into rational thinking that anything so seemingly irrational as dreams is dismissed as unreal and therefore irrelevant. In other words, our society programs us not to take dreams seriously. It teaches us to regard dream analysis and interpretation as holdovers from a less sophisticated and more superstitious age.

In many segments of the church today a reawakening has begun to the reality of dreams and dream language as a way that God communicates with His people. What is needed is the creation within the entire Body of Christ of a culture for revelation. God's people need to be taught to expect revelation through visionary means to become a matter of course in their Christian walk. Such a culture must be created in the church before it can spread to the rest of society.

The purpose of this chapter is to establish a framework for creating such a culture. With this in mind, let's begin by examining some of the ways and reasons we lose our dreams. We need to learn to recognize and overcome dream *snatchers*, dream *drainers*, and dream *busters*.

Dream Snatchers

One of the main reasons we lose dreams is because we have an enemy who is always waiting to snatch away and steal the revelation that the Holy Spirit brings to us through dreams. Let's be clear about this: the devil is a thief and a liar. He will do everything he can to rob us of our dream revelation. He will try to convince us that our dream is meaningless or that God will not speak to us that way. Sometimes he will even try to plant some insidious lie in its place.

Jesus said, *"The thief comes only to steal and kill and destroy; I came that they may have life, and have it abundantly."*[70] That is the devil's only goal: to steal, kill, and destroy the works of God, the people of God, and God's revelation to His people. Jesus, on the other hand, came to give abundant life. He came to *"destroy the works of the devil."*[71] This includes restoring us to a place where we can readily receive visionary revelation to the Holy Spirit.

Jesus had some other telling things to say about this "thief": *"But be sure of this, that if the head of the house had known at what time of the night the thief was coming, he would have been on the alert and would not have allowed his house to be broken into"; [72] "Truly, truly, I say to you, he who does not enter by the door into the fold of the sheep, but climbs up some other way, he is a thief and a robber." [73]*

Robbers usually prefer the dead of night for carrying out their dirty work. Darkness makes it easier for them to sneak in and surreptitiously steal valuable possessions from right under the owner's nose. This is the devil's preferred *modus operandi.* As the prince of darkness, he would rather remain in the shadows and lay an ambush than attack in the open.

We must realize that throughout the ages the devil and the powers of darkness have made an assault against believers in an attempt to snuff out the gifts of the Holy Spirit and the revelatory realms of God. The thief has been hard at work to steal the true power of the Holy Spirit and raise up a counterpart movement under the influence of the occult. But Jesus has prevailed and always will prevail through His people. The thief will be exposed, caught, and made to repay!

Proverbs 6:31 says that when a thief is caught "he must repay sevenfold," even to "all the substance of his house." What does this mean with regard to the spirit of revelation? This thief, the devil, seeks to steal from us the spirit of revelation, illumination, and dream language that God has released to us. Strictly speaking, if we enforce Jesus' victory on Calvary, when the devil steals one dream we must get seven in return! How do you feel about the idea of receiving a sevenfold increase in dreams, visions, and revelatory language?

It is time for us—indeed, for the whole church—to move into a higher dimension of the gifting of discerning of spirits and thus identify and capture the thief. Then we must enter into judicial intercession in a courtroom hearing and call forth retribution where God's judgment is released and retribution occurs.

But how can we ward off this thief in our daily lives? How can we prevent him from stealing our dreams even today? James provides us with a simple answer: *"Submit therefore to God. Resist the devil and he will flee from you." [74]* Basically it is a three-step process: (1) submit to God; (2) resist the devil; and (3) the devil will flee from you. The order of these steps is critically important! Don't try to resist the devil if you have not submitted your mind, will, and spirit to God; you will lose every time.

Submit to God; live in humble daily dependence on Him. Then and only then will you be able to resist the devil in the power of God and watch him run away in terror.

Dream Drainers

The devil is not the only enemy of our dreams that we have to watch out for. Every day we face any number of environments, attitudes, or circumstances that can drain away our dreams. Let me suggest that you perform a self-examination by considering the following questions.

Have You Inherited a Wrong Church Culture and Worldview?

Perhaps the most significant of the influences that can drain away our dreams is the church culture and worldview that many of us have inherited. As I mentioned earlier, throughout most of its history the church has officially disapproved and discounted dreams as a valid or trustworthy avenue for receiving divine revelation. Wrong traditions, theology, and worldviews have stolen the relevance of dreaming. We have erred and moved away from our Hebraic foundation and shifted into a Greek mind-set.

The wedding of Christian theology and Greek philosophy began with Augustine in the 4th century and culminated with Thomas Aquinas in the 13th century. Some good has come to the church from this joining. For one thing, it helped to provide a sound intellectual and rational basis for theology and the Christian faith. At the same time, however, it cast doubt on the validity of visionary experiences, considering them "irrational" (even though they are not) and therefore unreliable. "If dreams are 'irrational' and untrustworthy," (so goes this analytical mind-set) "then why pay attention to them at all?"

Psychologist, clergyman, and author Morton T. Kelsey describes perfectly the nature of the problem:

> There have been several reasons for paying little attention to dreams. But today the Christian neglect comes from one main reason. There is no place for the dream in the materialistic and logical scientism that has almost completely replaced the original thinking and philosophy of Christianity. This Aristotelian view, as proposed by Aquinas, refined by Descartes (and is taken as final truth by logical positivism), states quite simply that there

are only two realities. There is material reality and there is rational consciousness, and beyond this there is nothing else for humankind to know. This is just about as far as one can get from traditional Hebrew and Christian thought....

Thus the idea that any realm of nonphysical, nonrational reality makes contact with human beings is simply ruled out to begin with. There is no place for the dream to come from. Since dreams are certainly neither material nor rational, they must be merely the undigested bits of yesterday's physical sensations and thoughts, a rehash—and garbled at that. The fact that most dreams do not fit that description makes no difference. This is the only possible view of reality, and so the dream is rejected before it is allowed to speak.[75]

This joining of Greek and Hebrew thought inevitably produces a certain tension between the Greek mind-set with its emphasis on reason and logic and the Hebraic focus on the relational and the experiential. The church is heir to both the Greek and Hebrew traditions, and both are important—but they should be in balance. For centuries they have not been. Dreams and other visionary and experiential revelation have been in the background for far too long. It is time to restore the proper equilibrium to the Body of Christ.

Are You at Rest or Are You Striving?

If your mind and spirit are restless, you will find it hard to receive dream revelation. Scripture says, "*One handful of rest is better than two fists full of labor and striving after wind.*"[76] Isaiah wrote, "*For thus the Lord God, the Holy One of Israel, has said, 'In repentance and rest you will be saved, in quietness and trust is your strength.'*"[77]

Your ability to rest is critical for your ability to receive. *Rest is the incubation bed of revelation!* I am not talking so much about how many hours of sleep you get every night, although that can be important. I am talking about taking the time and developing the capacity to quiet your soul and rest in the Lord, waiting silently before Him.

Is Your Receptor Clean?

If you hope to receive revelation from the Lord, your channels of communication must be clean and uncluttered by the junk of the world. This involves renewing your mind. As Paul told the Ephesians:

Be renewed in the spirit of your mind, and put on the new self, which in the likeness of God has been created in righteousness and holiness of the truth. Therefore, laying aside falsehood, speak truth each one of you with his neighbor, for we are members of one another.[78]

We need to renew our minds and put on our new self, which has been fashioned in the likeness of God. Truthfulness at all times and in all things is the best way to keep your communication channel with God open.

Many things can clog the channel and make you unreceptive to God's voice. Some of the most common ones to watch out for are:

1. Worry. *"Cease from anger and forsake wrath; do not fret; it leads only to evildoing."*[79]

2. Anger. *"Be angry, and yet do not sin; do not let the sun go down on your anger, and do not give the devil an opportunity."*[80]

3. Lust. *"Love does no wrong to a neighbor; therefore love is the fulfillment of the law.... Let us behave properly as in the day, not in carousing and drunkenness, not in sexual promiscuity and sensuality, not in strife and jealousy. But put on the Lord Jesus Christ, and make no provision for the flesh in regard to its lusts."*[81]

4. Excess and addictions. *"And do not get drunk with wine, for that is dissipation, but be filled with the Spirit."*[82]

5. Bitterness. *"See to it that no one comes short of the grace of God; that no root of bitterness springing up causes trouble, and by it many be defiled."*[83]

Paul cautions us, *"Do not grieve the Holy Spirit of God, by whom you were sealed for the day of redemption."*[84] This is only a short list of the kinds of things that grieve the Holy Spirit; there are certainly many more. If you want to be a good receptor of dreams, you must keep your heart and mind pure, give no place to the devil, and do nothing to grieve the Holy Spirit.

Are You Wise Regarding Today's Entertainment?

You must be careful what you listen to because what you let in through your eyes and your ears is what your heart and mind will dwell on. Many western Christians, especially in America, severely lack discernment and discretion in this area. We have become so jaded by the constant bombardment of the worldly in our entertainment that we barely even notice it anymore. We have become desensitized not only to the impure things around us but also to the very need to keep our hearts and minds pure before God. We need a Pure Life Revolution! With this in mind, you might consider going on an entertainment fast! Purity is a magnet to revelation.

All revelation that God releases is pure because He is pure. Corruption occurs at our end. We all see the world and approach the things of God through the particular mental and spiritual "filters" that our life experiences and circumstances have put in place. All of these filters are different, and some are cleaner than others. Clean or dirty, they influence the way we see and respond to the world around us. More importantly, they affect the way we see and respond to God.

What filters are in place in your life? How clean are they? Do you filter life and revelation through love, joy, and peace or through anger, bitterness, and fear? Jesus said, "*Take care what you listen to. By your standard of measure it will be measured to you; and more will be given you besides.*"[85] And don't forget Paul's wise counsel: "*Finally, brethren, whatever is true, whatever is honorable, whatever is right, whatever is pure, whatever is lovely, whatever is of good repute, if there is any excellence and if anything worthy of praise, dwell on these things.*"[86] Be wise with your entertainment.

Are You Working With Your Routine?

Inconsistent schedules can hinder the flow and retention of revelation. Often this is not your fault but simply due to the demands of life. This is honestly the hardest one for me, due to my many travels. Cry out to the Lord, though, along with me for God's grace to help you to work with your schedule or even alter it if needed. Remember that my wife, Michal Ann, began receiving powerful dream revelation at night while asleep because the demands of life and four small children made it nearly impossible for her to get alone with God during the day on a consistent basis.

God will meet you where you are and work with you. Seek the Lord for special times that are set apart for receiving from Him. You may have to give up some things—even some good things—in order to obtain the best things. Sacrifice releases power. Occasional fasting can be helpful also because it will tenderize your heart and posture you for heavenly downloads.

Are You One to Whom Much Is Given?

In other words, have you proven to be faithful with a little so that God knows He can trust you with more? Sometimes we get impatient and want to progress more quickly than we are ready for. We yearn to receive great and abundant revelation from the Lord and become frustrated and discouraged when it doesn't come. It takes time to develop the integrity and maturity of character to handle dream revelation properly. God will not place on you more than you can bear. Prove faithful with a little, and God will give you more.

In explaining to His disciples why He talked to the people in parables, Jesus said, *"For whoever has, to him more shall be given, and he will have an abundance; but whoever does not have, even what he has shall be taken away from him."*[87] He then explained that He taught in parables because people whose hearts were spiritually dull and whose eyes and ears were closed would see but not perceive and hear but not understand. People whose hearts were open to the truth, on the other hand, *would* see and hear and understand. Then He concluded with these words: "But blessed are your eyes, because they see; and your ears, because they hear."[88]

God is always looking for people to whom He can entrust His revelation. He may test us with a little to see what we do with it. If we do not pay attention to what we have already received, the Holy Spirit is not obligated to give us more. Don't despise or degrade what the Lord gives you just because you feel it is only a little. Treat that little as the precious treasure it is. Prove faithful with that little, and God will entrust more to you. Faithfulness has its reward: increase!

Do You Have the Integrity to Handle God's Dream Revelation?

Integrity is a major issue in society today and especially in the church. Be very careful how you handle the revelation God gives you. People and the Holy Spirit both are drawn to integrity. Tomorrow's call does not give you authority today! There is a learning process of being called, trained, and commissioned (and *retrained* and *recommissioned!*). Don't distort the meaning of a dream out of your insecurity. Don't say more than God says, or more than God said to say. Don't add "hamburger helper" and thus exceed your level of credibility. Learn to pray and hold—do not cheat—and watch how you say it! God always ultimately has to judge pride!

Dream Busters[89]

Some enemies of our dream revelation come from the outside, worm their way in, and wield a negative influence on our minds. I call these "dream busters." They are the "Big 4 Ds": distraction, disinformation, disbelief, and the downward spiral.

Distraction

This one is a given in our busy, fast-paced lifestyle today. If you are having a cell phone conversation with someone while trying to do three other things, chances are you will not absorb everything that was intended in that call. There are many good things to do in life, but if we want to receive and retain revelation, then we will have to weed the garden of "distractions." This is one of the primary reasons why Scripture exhorts us to set our minds on *"things above"* and not on things of this earth.[90] If you can capture *"the little foxes that spoil the vine,"*[91] you will be amazed at what all God has to say to you! Cultivate times in your daily routine and schedule when you can get quiet before God, calm your mind from mundane distractions, and listen to Him.

Disinformation

Are you missing out on dream revelation because you have been the victim of disinformation? What does God have to say in His Word? Does God still speak today? Or has the false teaching of cessationism distorted your view? Too often as Christians we look to institutions, denominations, and uninformed people to get our theology rather than basing it on the Word of God. This is why many people do not believe God speaks to them today—not because of anything the Bible actually says, but what others wrongly *say* that it says! Consider this warning from Hosea: "My people are destroyed for lack of knowledge. Because you have rejected knowledge, I also will reject you from being My priest. Since you have forgotten the law of your God, I will also forget your children."[92]

Disinformation can be disastrous. If we are not taught properly, then neither will our children be taught properly because we will pass along our ignorance to them. And it will be worse in their generation because disinformation compounds. Wrong information and a lack of information feed a culture that allows the darkness of doubt to breed and remain.

Disbelief

Eventually, enough disinformation results in disbelief. Many people cannot and will not hear the voice of the Holy Spirit in their lives because they simply do not believe that God wants to speak to them in a personal way! They may believe that God still speaks in some form or fashion, or that He speaks through the Bible *only*, but they do not believe that He wants to speak to them on an individual basis.

Disbelief can filter out God's love, care, revelation, and, at times, even His empowerment. We must remember that we serve an all-powerful, all-knowing God who has spoken, is speaking, and will continue to speak to His people. If we have fallen into unbelief, then our first step should be to cry out, "*I do believe; help my unbelief!*"[93]

Downward Spiral

Left unchecked, distractions, disinformation, and disbelief will pull us into a downward spiral. As author and prophetic statesman Chuck Pierce explains it:

> Satan always will attempt to thwart God's plans. Such was the case for the Israelites. When they were coming out of their captivity in Babylon, they received a revelation from the Lord (see Jer. 29:10). The Israelites knew God's will for them was to return and rebuild the destroyed Temple of the Lord. They had heard clearly but as they began working toward the restoration God had for them, the enemy resisted their efforts. Instead of fighting for what they knew they were to do, the children of Israel gave in. As the people allow the enemy to take a foothold, three things happened.
>
> 1. **They fell into *discouragement*.** They began to ask why God was calling them to rebuild the Temple in the first place.
>
> 2. **They fell into *disillusionment*.** Things weren't going well, so they began to wonder if God had really told them to build at all.
>
> 3. **They fell into *disinterest*.** As the situation progressed, they decided they would build their own houses and leave His in disrepair. They stopped caring.

This progression of events is often a pattern for what can happen in our own lives if we do not guard what the Lord has told us and seriously pursue His will. It takes an act of our own will to choose God's plan for possessing our inheritance.[94]

Is your receptivity to dream language being hindered by distractions, disinformation, or disbelief? Are you in a downward spiral of discouragement, disillusionment, or disinterest? If so, you don't have to stay there. Getting off the downward spiral is never easy but neither is it impossible. God's plan and desire for all His children is that we be receptacles of His revelatory communication. Take action to possess your inheritance. Make a deliberate decision to reject those things that are holding you back. Choose God's plan. Through prayer and determined effort and with the help of the Holy Spirit, you *can* reverse the trend and end the downward spiral!

Dream Catchers

I want to be a *dream catcher* and I am sure this is the echo of your heart as well! Dream catchers create their own culture. Sometimes we have to fight to enter God's destiny for our lives, as so many forces in the world work against us every step of the way. Don't expect it to be a steady move forward like an irresistible storm surge. As in every other area of growth, your journey into the revelatory will have its ebb and flow and its ups and downs. Sometimes you will feel as though you are on a roller coaster. This is normal. Don't fret over it. Just keep pressing forward.

Why is dreaming so important? Why should we be so concerned about receiving dream revelation from the Lord? Because dream revelation is one of the ways that God can transfer His divine plan and intention to earthly reality. In so doing, He invites us to become involved with Him in His plan.

According to author and instructor Dr. Mark Rutland:

To receive a dream is the human obligation that begins to move the divine purpose from the mind of God to become reality in human history. God originates the greatest dreams of mankind and grants them as a special grace to the fearless and the faithful. To be open to dreaming His dreams is to be open to the very mind of God.

God is a dreamer who envisioned every microscopic detail of the universe before He spoke the first word of Creation. Now He summons us into that creative work, to dream and speak and bring forth that which we dream. Into holy hearts and sanctified imaginations God gives dreams that stir to action undaunted dreamers who, like their heavenly Father, envision what others cannot begin to imagine.

If God is a dreamer, which He is, and if He loves dreamers, which He does, then how precious to Him must be those who nurture dreams and dreamers. No mission more productive can be imagined than the raising up of dreamers. One who dreams his own dream does a mighty thing. Those who empower and unleash an army of dreamers are the divine multiplicand of kingdom arithmetic.[95]

Can you grasp the awesome nature of this? God, a Creator by nature, is still at work doing a majestic thing and He wants to use your life, your gifts, and your capabilities in His creative work in the earth today! Let yourself go! Dream with God!

Pull Out Your Spiritual Antenna

In order to do that, you must become a good receptor. Just as you have to pull out your antenna in order to receive sound transmissions, you must pull out your spiritual antenna so you can receive God's transmissions. Get ready! Expect to receive!

The great 19th-century British preacher Charles Spurgeon once received an entire sermon in a dream. He preached it aloud, and his wife, who was awake, wrote it down. Later, he preached the message from the pulpit to great effect. If God did it then, He can do it again! Over here, right now! Expect great things from God!

Apply the Blood of Jesus

Just as a radio transmitter/receiver needs electrical power in order to function, we need spiritual power for our spiritual antenna to work. That power comes from the blood of Jesus. There is an old gospel hymn that says, "There is power, power, wonder-working power in the blood of the Lamb." The writer of the Book of Hebrews states it as follows:

But when Christ appeared as a high priest of the good things to come, He entered through the greater and more perfect tabernacle, not made with hands, that is to say, not of this creation; and not through the blood of goats and calves, but through His own blood, He entered the holy place once for all, having obtained eternal redemption.[96]

Jesus has attained the place for us to be able to come into the very holy presence of God Himself. So, if you want to dream, try applying the blood of Jesus in your life. He is your power source. Don't worry if you don't have great spiritual discipline. That can come with practice and experience. But as a child of God you *do* have great spiritual *privileges.* Apply the blood of Jesus on the doorposts of your heart and mind and bring them into alignment with His will and purpose.

Pray in the Spirit

Another way to prepare yourself to become a dream catcher is by learning to pray in the Spirit. Build yourself up in your faith by *"praying in the Holy Spirit."*[97] This is an amazing and underutilized gift! God promises to give us refreshment, the stirring of our faith, and an atmosphere where mysteries are spoken and revealed. Get yourself ready! Praying in the gift of tongues is not the least of the gifts; it is often the entrance into all the gifts. Strengthen your spirit man. Charge your batteries of faith by praying in the Holy Spirit!

Meditate on the Word of God

A fourth key to dream catching is to meditate on the Word of God. "This book of the law shall not depart from your mouth, but you shall meditate on it day and night, so that you may be careful to do according to all that is written in it; for then you will make your way prosperous, and then you will have success."[98]

To meditate on God's Word means to take a small portion—a verse, a sentence, a phrase, or even perhaps a single word—and ponder it, turn it over in your mind every which way, and ruminate on it like a cow chewing its cud. That is literally what it means to meditate. (I address this subject in much greater detail in my book: *The Lost Art of Practicing His Presence.* In it there is a whole chapter on Christian Meditative Prayer.)

Go on the journey with me. It is a joy! It is a privilege. It is one of His ways. Meditate on the Word of God and the God of the Word!

Worship Extravagantly

Finally, if you want to become a good dream catcher, then become a passionate worshiper. Jesus said that the Father is looking for people who will worship Him "in spirit and truth."[99] Worshiping the Lord in spirit and truth will put your heart and mind in a proper spiritual posture to receive His revelation. He will also go ahead of you in triumph as your enemies are put under your feet.

> Jehoshaphat bowed his head with his face to the ground, and all Judah and the inhabitants of Jerusalem fell down before the Lord, worshiping the Lord. The Levites…stood up to praise the Lord God of Israel, with a very loud voice. …Jehoshaphat stood and said, "Listen to me, O Judah and inhabitants of Jerusalem, put your trust in the Lord your God and you will be established. Put your trust in His prophets and succeed." When he had consulted with the people, he appointed those who sang to the Lord and those who praised Him in holy attire, as they went out before the army and said, "Give thanks to the Lord, for His lovingkindness is everlasting." When they began singing and praising, the Lord set ambushes against the sons of Ammon, Moab and Mount Seir, who had come against Judah; so they were routed.[100]

Watch out for the enemy. Don't let that thief snatch away your dreams. Don't let erroneous teaching rob you of your inheritance. Rest in the Lord. Keep your receptor clean. Be wise and discerning about what you watch and listen to. Work with your routine. Be faithful with what you have so that you will receive more. Maintain your integrity. Don't let distractions, disinformation, and disbelief put you on the downward spiral to discouragement, disillusionment, and disinterest.

Pull out your spiritual antenna. Trust in the power of the blood of Jesus. Pray in the Spirit. Meditate on the Word of God. Worship passionately. Then you too will become a dream catcher! You will create for yourself, your family, and others around you a culture of light, spiritual power, and revelation. Your passion for the Lord will create a magnetic draw and attract the Holy Spirit, and watch what happens! You too will be a dream catcher!

Reflection Questions

1. What are some of the Dream Snatchers and Dream Drainers mentioned in this chapter?

2. According to Chuck Pierce, what are the three steps toward a downward spiral?

3. How can you become a Dream Catcher? What are some practical steps?

Referral Readings

Mark Rutland, *Dream* (Lake Mary, FL: Charisma House, 2003).

John and Paula Sandford, *The Elijah Task* (Plainsfield, NJ: Logos International, 1974).

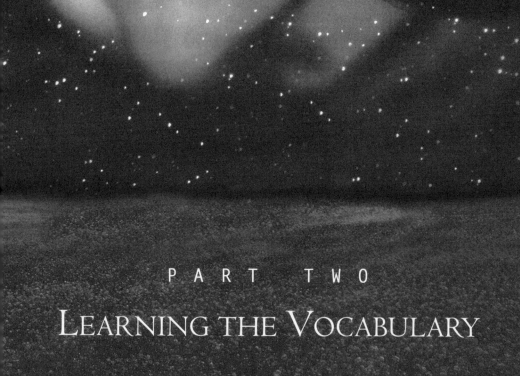

PART TWO

LEARNING THE VOCABULARY

One-third of your life is spent in the dream world, and while your body rests, your subconscious is actively involved in dreaming. Dreaming is not exactly like the language you use in your conscious world where you deal in the objective world of facts and figures. In the dream world the language is more spiritual and symbolic, and if you are not learned in this heavenly dream language then you will misinterpret the meaning.

In Part Two, I will provide some instruments of interpretation that will help you understand the dream language so that you can capture its full-intended content. You will learn that you do not have to drift alone in your attempts to understand the mysteries of dream language. Jesus has already sent you the Holy Spirit to be your personal guide through the complex maze of the dream world, thus teaching you the spiritual alphabet of the dream language.

Dream interpretation is like a giant jigsaw puzzle with thousands of tiny pieces that must be fitted together in exactly the right order. The quickest way to complete a jigsaw puzzle is to start with the border, the framework. The same is true with dream interpretation. In the first part of the book I helped to create a framework for interpreting your dreams, and now in this part I will help you to complete the framework. Before long, the big picture will begin to take shape.

As dreams invade our inner life, they work to encourage, exhort, direct, correct, inspire, cleanse, and direct us. In order for your dreams to work to their fullest, you must learn the vocabulary of dreams, and then their message will move from mystery to clarity. Continue on the journey with me as we continue to learn our new the vocabulary.

CHAPTER FIVE

DREAMS WORK!
(BY MICHAL ANN GOLL)

There were two pivotal points in time where the Lord changed my life, through the supernatural activity of dreams! The first major point of impact dealt with healing my fractured perception of God my Father, in relation to myself. The second impartation took me to a much deeper place. In this place I went beyond my needs, my perceptions. The Lord allowed me to see His aching heart for His Bride. I felt the urgency of the need for His Body to wake up and love Him, know Him, and recognize Him.

This second download was not the warm and fuzzy, "climb into the lap of your Papa" experience. It was fearful and terrifying, as though our gentle Papa unzipped a small portion of His "superman" suit and shafts of His glory and brilliance streamed out. He released angelic warriors to visit my bedroom, bringing with them fireballs, and touching me with hot, sizzling bolts of electricity! My personal dream journey has been a wild and exciting ride! As dramatic as some of these experiences have been, I would not trade them for anything! I thank the Lord for meeting me right where I was, insecure and broken, and bringing healing to me. But He didn't stop there. He took me beyond myself and turned my gaze outward—to see Him, and the need, the pain of His heart.

Being a wife and mother is an awesome privilege, bringing great fulfillment and contentment. However, it also brings with it long days and short nights, filled with always needing to care for someone or something, endless "to do" lists, and the ever circling "What's for dinner?" question that seems to creep up on you as the day quickly slips through your fingers. This was the practical world I was living in, while at the same time, I was longing for my spiritual walk with God to deepen and grow. He took my "time-cramped, impossible" situation, and breathed His creative swirl of release, and changed me from a longing, hurting, but at the same time faithful, loyal housewife and mother of four small children to a Holy Spirit-charged woman of vision and power, secure and whole.

At this point you may be thinking, "Okay, all this dream stuff sounds pretty good, but is it for real? Do dreams really *work?* Will God really speak to me in my dreams? Can I really walk in the realm of dream language and revelation?"

My answer to you is, "Yes! Absolutely!" In the Book of Joel, God promises that He will visit His people with dreams and visions. He is not a respecter of persons. If you are hungry as I was and willing to do what it takes to "prepare your vessel," create a culture for revelation, and become a dream catcher, then God will speak to you too.

In this chapter, let's go on a little journey together. I'd like to share with you some of the dreams the Lord has given to me, dreams that have been woven into the very fabric of my life.

Tornadoes and Bears

Over the years God has given me so much in the realm of dreams. Although my immersion into the world of revelatory divine dreaming dramatically accelerated in the late 1980s and 1990s, my dream journey actually began many years earlier. I was an active dreamer as a child. Unfortunately, many of my dreams were nightmares. As I reflect on those early dream experiences, those childhood nightmares seemed generally to have centered around two themes: tornadoes and bears.

I remember having dreams in which huge tornadoes would come at me from every direction. It was as though these storms had a mental capacity to track me. They seemed to always know my position, know if and where I was hiding, and know exactly where I was going. I could never get away from them. It was the same way with the dreams about bears. They were always after me. These dreams were so frequent and so terrifying that I came to the point where I was afraid to go to bed at night. I was afraid to go to sleep. I was afraid to dream.

Later on I learned that certain types of dreams sometimes have generational roots. For example, one day my mother told me that she also had dreams of tornadoes. There were four children in our family, and she often dreamed that three of us were safe in the shelter with her while the one was outside somewhere. Even as the tornado approached, she would go outside and search for the missing child.

When my mother shared this story with me, a little light bulb turned on in my mind, and I realized, "This is a generational issue." It got even more interesting one Christmas when our entire family gathered at that century-old farmhouse where I had been raised. My nephew, who was three years old at the time, was asleep in *my old bedroom*. In the middle of the night he woke up screaming, saying, "The wind is going to get me! The wind is going to get me!"

As Jim and I processed this issue of generational dreams about tornadoes, it seemed as though there was a place of vulnerability that allowed entrance for those types of dreams. We had to come before the Lord, plead the blood of Jesus, and cut off the spirit of fear attached to those dreams.

We also discovered that there is a redemptive way to look at the focus of those same dreams. For example, tornadoes can be very destructive, but a tornado in a dream can also symbolize the violent activity of God when He comes and shakes everything up. He rips out and demolishes the old dead stuff because He wants to bring in the new. He wants to impart life. God wants to shake up our understanding of what Christianity is supposed to look like. Sometimes God decides it is time to clean house. Looking at it from this paradigm gives a whole new perspective to tornado dreams.

This is, in fact, a picture of what God has done in my own life. He came in with His swirling tornadic activity and shook every part of my life that could be shaken. He threw out the old stuff, brought in the new, and rearranged my "house," purifying me in the process. What the enemy meant for evil, God turned into good. As Mahesh Chavda once prophesied to Jim and I, we are called to be "storm chasers."

As for the bears? Jim and I have always carried in our hearts a burden for the Jews in Russia to be released from that country. The bear is a symbol for Russia. Could it be that the Lord was touching a future call in my life? I sure think so!

So you see, there are times when you can look through the eyes of redemption and see things differently. You can get a fuller perspective of what is really going on when you view it from God's vantage point.

Colorado Deliverance

After Jim and I married, we decided for one of our early vacations to drive to Colorado and camp out in a little pup tent. We were living in the Kansas City area at the time. Camping is not really our thing, but money was tight at that time and camping seemed an inexpensive way to have a vacation together.

The place where we camped was beautiful, but I had trouble relaxing and enjoying it. I was still bound up in my childhood fears stemming from my nightmares. In that wilderness location all I could think about was bears. My mind filled with images of bears rampaging through our campground, ripping up our tent, and eating our food (and us too, maybe!). I kept telling myself, "This will be fun. We'll have a great time. I will be brave. I'm a grown woman; I can *do* this." A park ranger even assured us that no bears had been sighted in that area for about 15 years. Yet despite all these assurances, my fear still simmered.

I thought I had my fear under control, until night came and we crawled into the pup tent. There in the dark, in that tiny tent, my fear of bears suddenly overwhelmed me. I could not get away from it and was quickly becoming unglued. Finally, I said, "Jim, I can't do this. I need some help. I need you to pray for me."

Jim immediately responded and kicked into prayer mode. He bound the spirit of fear of bears and the spirit of fear of tornadoes and cast them out of me. Short and simple, to the point! After that, I never had another moment of fear concerning those issues. The enemy tried to bind me, but the Lord broke those bonds and set me free.

I share this to encourage any of you who struggle with a similar fear. Do you, your children, or your grandchildren—or maybe all three generations—struggle with nightmares or sudden terror in the night? Do your nightmares seem to center around a common theme or two that transcends generations? You can be free of the fear. The Lord will set you free. He does not want you to live in fear of your dreams. He wants to place you in a mental and emotional posture where you can readily receive His dream revelation.

Before reading any further, take a moment to bring your fear to the Lord. Let me suggest that you pray the following prayer, or something similar, and find freedom:

> Father, I come to You in Jesus' name. I call upon Your anointing and upon the blood of Jesus to cancel this curse. I say no to nightmares—no more bad dreams. In the name of Jesus I call for a release right now, a cutting off of generational fears. By the authority of Jesus' name I say that my sleep and the sleep of those I love will be sweet and free from torment by terror or fear. Lord, release Your redemptive work in our lives so that instead of terror we will be filled with Your Spirit in the night. I call forth Your purpose and Your destiny to be released in us and let it unfold through our dreams. In the name of Jesus, Amen.

Welcome, Holy Spirit

I'm a country girl by upbringing. The rural Methodist church where I grew up had a typical Sunday attendance of 12-16, including our family of six. Our family did practically everything at the church: taught Sunday school, played the piano, took up the offering, kept a key to the church. In the wintertime, my father would drive to the church on Saturday night and light the fire in the stove so the building would be warm in the morning. We were very down home, and very small, but we loved God very much.

I loved God. I also loved the Holy Spirit; I just did not know how powerful He was. At that time I knew nothing about the baptism in the Holy Spirit. I just kept saying, "Holy Spirit, I want You." Then I met Jim. Even though he was only 23, he was already a ministry leader.

Jim and I met while we were both working at a hospital over one summer. We became good friends and loved talking about the Lord, praying for patients after work, and just working together. We had an unusual courtship, as the Lord spoke to both of us, strongly and clearly, that we were to be married. We were best friends at this point. Suddenly,

I was thrust into a world unlike any I had ever known. Here I was, a country girl from a tiny country church, engaged to a man who was already moving powerfully in the gifts of the Spirit. He was prophesying over people; people were being delivered; evangelism was taking place all over the college campus.

I looked at Jim and the circles he was already moving in, and I felt very intimidated. Now I was to be married to a pastor who was also highly prophetic. I began to feel pressure that I needed to minister to people in the same way, with the same gifting, as my soon-to-be husband.

Fear is such an awful power. It attempts to surround you, isolate you, and cut you off from those you need the most. I was insecure, and in my insecurity I began to make the wrong equation that giftedness equals relationship. I felt the necessity to run by Jim any revelation I had received. For example, we would be praying together, and I would feel the Holy Spirit speak to me about something and I would bring it to Jim. If the Holy Spirit had not spoken it to Jim, I assumed that I had heard incorrectly. I discarded what the Lord had given me and went with whatever Jim thought. Before long, I subordinated my own revelatory experiences and began to ride Jim's spiritual coattails.

Do you know what happens when you do that? You begin losing your own ability to hear the Lord. Your sensitivity to His voice decreases. You start to lose your bearings, and your life becomes unfocused and directionless. Being able to hear the Lord's voice is such an integral part of our relationship with Him. Indeed, it is indispensable. Unless we hear God's voice, how will we know what He wants us to do or where He wants us to go?

Eventually, the Lord began dealing with my heart on this issue. One night we were in a prayer meeting, and I felt like the Lord had given me a song. Before this, anytime I felt I had received a message from God, I would always reach over, elbow Jim, and say, "I think I have a song from the Lord. What do you think?" Jim always encouraged me. He never put me down or said, "Oh, this is not the right time." He always said, "Yeah, do it."

But this time, just as I was ready to nudge Jim again with my elbow, I heard the Lord say to me, "Is he your God, or am I?" The question was so loud and so clear that I repented on the spot. In an instant, I realized how my hearing of His voice had been lessened because I was placing the voice and opinion of others ahead of those of the Lord. God taught me a huge lesson that night. You can't equate gifting with relationships. And for me, this whole area of dreams is all about relationships—most importantly, your relationship to your Father!

Some years later I had a dramatic deliverance from intimidation, which was very powerful and very dramatic! From that point on I kept walking farther and farther into His light and getting rid of my fear and the other different things that were hindering me from the full life He wanted for me. Since that deliverance, the Lord has used me time and again to break off fear and intimidation from countless other lives. What a blast to be able to free people from bondages similar to those you have been captive to! Awesome!

Life in the Basement

A few years later we were in the process of building a new house. Having already sold our current house, we had to move out before the new house was finished. Because of this, we spent three months living in another family's basement. At this time we had four children. I was home schooling the oldest, who was six, and two of the three younger children were still in diapers. Jim was busy traveling here and there to various conferences and meetings, speaking and doing ministry, especially on weekends.

It was normal after one of these weekends for Jim to arrive home, walk in the door, and start talking about how good God was. He would talk about how the Holy Spirit had shown up in great power and how the prophetic words just came and how this and that happened. All the while I'm standing there with an armload of home schooling books, next to a load of diapers that needed folding. Outside I was all smiles: "That's wonderful, Jim!" Inside I was saying, "I don't want to hear it. Don't tell me about another great meeting." I felt left out and definitely shortchanged.

The longer this went on the more frustrated and jealous I became. In addition to the home schooling and the children, with Jim gone so often I also had to oversee the ongoing progress in building our house. Added to that was the stress of living in someone else's basement and trying to keep four small children fairly quiet.

One day, after hearing another amazing God-story from Jim's latest big escapade, I leaned my head against the wall in the hallway and began to cry. I didn't even say anything; my tears were my silent prayers to the Lord. He knew exactly where I was. At that moment He came to me and said, "Ann, what is impossible with man is possible with God. I am going to come and start visiting you in the night seasons."

Viruses From the Pit No More!

Now He had given me dreams before, but this was a significant increase in the presence of the Lord coming to me. I was like a computer infected with all sorts of bad viruses: viruses of comparison, rejection, insufficiency—you name it. Every night the Holy Spirit came and ran His divine "spy ware" to remove those viruses from the "hard drive" of my heart and mind. He did it night by night and He did it through dream language. Here are a couple of my favorites.

The Old Man at the Piano

I have always loved to sing. When I was growing up, however, few in my family ever really thought of me as a singer. In fact, I thought they probably preferred me to be quiet! One of my three brothers is very gifted musically. He was the one everybody wanted to listen to. So I used to go out on one of the far fields of our 120-acre farm and sing at the top of my voice to my heart's content. After all, I wasn't singing to please people; I was communing with the Lord.

One night I had a dream of a big family gathering. All my relatives were there, sitting around the kitchen table drinking coffee and telling old family stories. I was in the kitchen helping my mother serve dessert. Everybody was having a great time.

Meanwhile, an old gentleman was outside sitting at a piano, beside a beautiful warm fire, holding auditions. Everyone in the house was buzzing, certain that my musical brother would get the part. After all, he was the singer of the family. I too was confident that he would get it.

Different ones went out to audition. Upon their return, they came into the kitchen and said, "Michal Ann, you really ought to go out and sing for him." Like Martha in the New Testament, I was too busy serving to go out. In reality, my problem was disbelief. I simply could not believe that anyone would want *me* to audition. I kept saying that I would, but my heart was not in it. So instead, I hid my disbelief behind my work.

Everybody was waiting for my musically talented brother to go out, confident that he would win the role. Even he thought so. He went out full of confidence but came back in shaking his head and saying, "I can't believe it! I didn't get the part!"

Finally, there was no one else to audition and no more work to be done in the kitchen. Everybody was saying, "Michal Ann, it is your turn now. He is waiting for you. He wants you to come out."

Bowing to the pressure, I went outside. But I had no idea what to sing. The old gentleman was seated at the piano, patiently waiting. Having thought of a song, I began singing. I had only gotten a few measures into the song when he stopped me. "No," he said gently, "that's not it. Let's try it again." He was changing my whole singing paradigm. I was singing out of my head, and he was trying to get me to sing from deep within—from my heart.

I tried another song. Once again he stopped me. "No, that's still not it. Try again." I began to make the transition from my head to my heart. I opened my mouth, took a deep breath—but had no idea what I was going to sing. Suddenly, it came bubbling up from deep within. The old gentleman looked at me and said, "Yes! That's it. You've got it."

This dream revolutionized my life. It shifted my placement in the Spirit. It was a spiritual impartation that lifted me out of unbelief and a sense of inferiority and into a deeper divine relationship with the Lord. I was auditioning for Him, and it didn't make any difference what anybody else thought.

Walking Down a Country Lane

I had a second dream in which the same old gentleman and I were walking down a country lane. It was a beautiful fall afternoon. Tall trees lined either side of the lane, and their branches reached over to form a leafy canopy over our heads. As we walked, neither of us said a word. It was one of those times of close communion when the two of you are so in tune that you know what each other is thinking and feeling without exchanging audible words.

After a little while we stopped, and I had the clear impression that he wanted me to reach up and embrace him, because he loved the fragrance of my hair. And even walking side by side it was as though we were not close enough. He loved the fragrance of my hair and had waited so long that he just couldn't stand it anymore and got closer to me.

All the while I was thinking, "Why would anyone want to smell my hair?" It just seemed so foolish to me because I had never experienced anything like that before. Yet in this dream I felt the incredible love that my heavenly Father had for me and realized how deeply and intimately He knew me. He knew every part of me and, better still, loved every part of me. He knew me better than I knew myself. This dream imparted assurance, comfort, and a deeper knowledge of the love of God as my Father.

Dream Eggs

Night after night the Lord came to me with such incredibly sweet dreams, building me up and undoing rejection and fear and comparison and all those kinds of things. I like to call my dreams "dream eggs" because most of the time I do not receive the interpretation for them right away. Like other eggs, dream eggs need time and warmth to develop and hatch. I envision it this way: a large nest full of little eggs that I am responsible to incubate. In prayer I will go to those different eggs and pick them up, turn them over, and offer them to the Lord. Every now and then one of them hatches, and I get to see what it is. I have many eggs that still have not hatched, but I still turn them over. I still tend them carefully, believing that God will hatch each one when its time comes.

Of course, there is so much more to dreams than simply interpreting them and understanding what they mean. Dreams can lead us to the heart of the Father. You can receive the most awesome dream, record it in your journal, and even spend hours pondering its meaning, but if it does not draw you closer to the Lord, you have missed the most important point of all.

Dream language awakens your heart and activates childlike faith where you know that with God anything is possible. Dream big dreams! Let these God-sized dreams explode out of you and affect virtually every area of your life.

Nighttime dreams can be extremely powerful for a couple of reasons. First, when we are asleep we are free from distractions, and the Lord can have the undivided attention of our resting minds. Second, all our barriers are down. All the defense mechanisms that we erect every day to protect ourselves from getting hurt are laid aside for a few hours. As we live there open and exposed, the Holy Spirit can instill a healing balm on our hearts and speak to us in a precious, unique, and personal way.

Dreams can also awaken our walk with God. In one of my dreams I saw field of flowers, so beautiful and colorful, so fresh and so close together that the field was literally covered with them. It was like a beautiful mural. I did not realize that the picture was covered with yellow cellophane until that coating was ripped off. Then I saw those flowers in their full glory, more beautiful than I had ever imagined, with colors brighter and more vivid than I would have thought possible! It was as though they were transformed from just being in a picture, to being infused with life and movement. And the fragrance! I had never smelled anything so wonderful! It seemed to me as though these flowers represented people who were releasing their fragrance to the Lord.

A strong wind mixed the individual aromas together into one powerful and unique fragrance, as though if any flower did not release its aroma the recipe for the ultimate mixing of the fragrance would be incomplete. This combined fragrance was so compelling that it drew the Lord down from Heaven. He smelled this awesome fragrance, and He said, "Oh, I must come down. I cannot wait any longer. This fragrance is compelling Me to come down!" The flowers were so thick that I saw nowhere for Him to put His feet without crushing some of those precious blossoms. But as His feet touched the ground and He began to carefully, tenderly walk, the flowers parted before Him. Each place He stepped, the petals lovingly and gently caressed His feet, each one taking turns to display their affection for Him, each one longing to touch Him.

Having lived for a time under the thumb of intimidation, I felt an identity with so many others being caught under a "yellow cellophane wrap" of control and "plastic life." I saw that God had given me a piece of insight. How could I leave so many under the same oppression? And, if I really wanted to have Jesus come and walk among us, I knew I needed my fellow brothers and sisters to be free—free to release His fragrance deposited within each of them. I saw that we have been afraid to stand out or to be too different. We dress like everyone else, laugh like every one else, talk like every one else. We are afraid to release too much fragrance because we don't want people to think we are weird. We've been bound up in religious "yellow cellophane," and you know, when you're under that weight, you can't breathe! What a delight it is to rip off that awful confinement and watch dear brothers and sisters breathe for the first time in a long time!

In another dream, I was at a conference where I heard the challenge, "Who will volunteer to be mothers and fathers in the prophetic?" There was a long line of men and women, shoulder to shoulder, who would be required to make a decision, either yes or no, concerning this challenge. I was in the line also. I had my eyes closed and I knew what my answer was going to be. I was determined not to budge. I wasn't moving anywhere. But, when I opened my eyes in the dream, I saw that everyone else had taken a step back and there I was, having volunteered in spite of myself. I tried to sit back down, but a group of women came up behind me, scooped me out of my chair, and sent me flying forward in the air. I think I've been flying ever since! Now my family and I actually live in Tennessee—the volunteer state. Yes, I volunteered!

Are Dreams for Everybody?

At the beginning of this chapter I asked the question, "Do dreams really work?" I hope by this time you see that they do. I also stated that if God speaks to me through dreams, He will speak to you. Does this mean that spiritual, revelatory dreams are for everybody? I believe they can be. The key is to come hungry enough to ask God to visit you in the night seasons and with an expectant faith that He will answer.

Psalm 127:2 says that God gives to His beloved ones even in their sleep. How many times have you had a dream, and when you woke up, it vanished? I can't begin to count all those instances. I used to get really upset about it, until this one day, when God gave me a new insight. One night when we were living in that basement, I had powerful dream that I wanted to make sure I remembered. I mentally catalogued it and was confident I had it. When I awoke again in the morning, I remembered my dream—for a few seconds. Then it was gone. It really frustrated me. I felt sure the enemy had come along and stolen my dream. I asked God to restore it. I asked Him to give me back the memory of my dream. He did. But here's the funny thing: as soon as He gave it back to me, He took it away again.

"Why did You do that, Lord?" I asked. "That was a really powerful dream." It was then that the Lord brought Psalm 127:2 to my mind, and I remembered that God gives to His beloved ones even in their sleep. I realized that just because I don't recall a dream doesn't mean that He did not give it to me.

How many times have you been in a situation where you had a sense of déjà vu? Everything looks strangely familiar, and you feel like you have been there before, even though you know you haven't. Our minds are like file cabinets. God gives us dreams in our sleep, but sometimes He files them away in the back of our mind where they are safe from being stolen by the enemy and where they can be pulled out again at an appropriate time. You may not remember the dream immediately afterward, but the day may come when you will receive a word of knowledge or a word of wisdom and suddenly the "knower" in you becomes activated. God pulls a long forgotten dream out of the file cabinet and opens it before your inner vision. God never wastes anything. If He gives you a dream, He has an amazing divine reason.

Just as you may not always recall all your dreams, you also may not receive an immediate interpretation for all of them. That is certainly the case with me. God gives us dreams for His own purposes. One of His main purposes is to draw us to Himself. I believe that one reason God does not always immediately grant interpretation to our dreams is because He is more interested in pursuing a love relationship with us than He is in our getting the right information. Having an unanswered question or an unsolved riddle often will drive us to pursue God in a greater way than if we had all of the answers. God loves to give us mysteries; He loves to give us questions that He does not seem to answer. That unknown factor stirs a hunger in us to draw closer. It is God's way of saying, "Come a little closer. Come a little closer, and ask Me again."

Receive a little perspective here. Sometimes I think the Lord likes to play hide and seek! He hides the revelation so we will seek after it. Usually, the answer doesn't come by just knocking at His door. He invites us to come in, sit down, have some refreshment together. As we connect heart to heart, He weaves a beautiful tapestry of gold and silver, threads of our lives woven with threads of His love and destiny. It is a priceless fabric, delicate but sturdy, glorious but also humble. His heart is that these threads become woven so tightly and securely together, that as this tapestry nears completion, we lose sight of the individual threads. We can't tell anymore where our threads begin and His end. In fact, as we grow in grace, love, and understanding, we stop trying to figure it out, and we say, "More of You, and less of me!"

Ah, now that's a dream come true! What a special, unique way God works with each one of us!

Reflection Questions

1. What inspiration can you take from Michal Ann's dream journey for your life?

2. What are the viruses that could be affecting your revelatory life in God?

3. What does Psalms 127:2 mean to you?

Referral Reading

Larry Randolph, *Spirit Talk* (Wilkesboro, NC: Morningstar Publications, 2005).

Michal Ann Goll, *Women on the Frontlines* (Shippensburg, PA: Destiny Image, 1999).

CHAPTER SIX

THE DIVERSITY OF DREAMS

Dreams are as diverse as the languages we speak, the clothing we wear, and the food we eat. Dreams are a communications expression of the creative heart of God. As the Master artistically paints each flower of the field, so dreams are individually tailor-made for you and me.

What are dreams made of? Are they spiritual gifts given for us to unwrap? Revelatory dreams naturally fall under the spiritual gift of prophecy. Yet they are too broad to be confined neatly and strictly just to one gift. Dreams may also be an impartation of the gift of discerning of spirits. Like the colors in a rainbow in overlapping shades, difficult to tell where one stops and another begins, dreams are definitely unique and creative expressions of spiritual gifts. There are no clear lines of demarcation between spiritual gifts. The word of wisdom blends into a word of knowledge. The gift of faith overlaps with the workings of miracles. Yes, dreams are spiritual gifts that intertwine with various enchanting shades.

As I said before, dream language is not a dead language but a dynamic, living language of love. The primary difference between dreams and other revelatory impartations is that we receive dreams first in our subconscious and only later become aware of them in our conscious minds. Because of the divine nature of revelation, we must depend on the Holy Spirit for understanding. Jesus said, *"When He, the Spirit of truth, comes, He will guide you into all the truth; for He will not speak on His own initiative, but whatever He hears, He will speak; and He will disclose to you what is to come."*[101]

As Creator, God is incredibly diverse. He loves variety. Just one look at the natural world in all its abundant variety is enough to show the diversity of God's creative nature. This diversity is just as true for the spiritual realm as for the natural. Paul wrote:

> *Now there are varieties of gifts, but the same Spirit. And there are varieties of ministries, and the same Lord. There are varieties of effects, but the same God who works all things in all persons. But to each one is given the manifestation of the Spirit for the common good.*[102]

There are diversities of spiritual giftings, but all come from the same Holy Spirit. Each of us as believers receives the manifestation of the Spirit, but in different grace packages and in a variety of ways. We are so different from one another. We think differently from each other and we perceive things in a different way. The Spirit of God tailors His impartations to match our individual callings. So, just as there are diversities of spiritual gifts, there are also diversities of dreams. The Holy Spirit matches our dreams to the way we think and perceive individually. In other words, He gives us dreams according to our sphere or realm of influence. It is part of His amazing nature.

Dreams According to Your Sphere

When the Holy Spirit gives you dreams and other types of supernatural encounters, He will do so according to the calling of God on your life. We receive according to our allotment or our sphere of influence. The Greek word is *metron*. Whether they are dreams about your home, your children, your workplace, your local church, city, or nation, you will receive dreams that relate to the sphere of influence you have in your life.

Because we each have different spheres of influence and callings, our revelation will differ from each other also—*not* conflicting or contradictory revelation, just different because of our different spheres. God never contradicts Himself and neither does His revelation.

For example, if your calling is to evangelism, your dreams will probably tend to be evangelistic in nature. If yours is a pastoral sphere, you will receive dreams of sheep and tending to the flock. If your gifting includes prophetic ministry, your dreams will be highly revelatory in nature. If you are called to the marketplace, then His creative means of communicating with you will address that arena. If you are in the health care profession, then your dreams will often speak of nurture, healing, and releasing love. If you work in government, your dreams will deal with spheres of authority. Each revelation will demonstrate a different level of impact and anointing. It all depends on your sphere.

Measure of Rule

Just as we each have a sphere of revelation, we each also have a *measure of rule* or influence. Part of our creation mandate from God is to exercise dominion over the created order. We have a stewardship to rule in the earth. The Holy Spirit determines our measure of rule according to the will of our heavenly Father, and it is different with each of us.

Our measure of delegated rule is determined by three elements: our measure of *gift*, our measure of *authority* and our measure of *faith*. These three elements combined help explain why some people seem to have a much greater sphere of influence than others. Some people have a sphere of influence that is global in scale. Most of us, however, operate on a smaller level such as our community or local congregation.

This does not mean that the ministries of people with smaller measures of rule are less important than larger ones. Don't fall into the comparison trap. Just because someone else's sphere may be larger than yours does not mean that God loves you or favors you any less than He does that other person. Remember, God never wastes anything. And He never acts without purpose.

The Lord determines our measure of rule according to His sovereign will and He gifts and equips us accordingly. Our measure of rule sets the boundaries for what God expects of us at any given time. In God's system of evaluation and reward, faithfulness is more important than volume. He promised that if we are faithful with a little He will give us much. The key is being faithful with what He *has* given us. Large, small or in between, our measure of rule and how we exercise it is very important to God. It is a crucial part of His overall redemptive purpose for humanity.

Within our measure of rule we each have a measure of *gift*, which refers to the specific level or degree of grace gifting we have received from the Holy Spirit. This measure will always be sufficient for the sphere of influence that God has given us. We also each have a measure of *authority* that defines our functional position and sphere of influence. Inside that arena of authority we will be highly effective; outside of that position our effectiveness and inpact will decrease. Paul recognized the scope of his sphere and was careful to stay inside it: *"But we will not boast beyond our measure, but within the measure of the sphere which God apportioned to us as a measure, to reach even as far as you."* [103]

Finally, the measure of *faith* describes the degree of confidence with which we move in our gift with authority: *"For through the grace given to me I say to everyone among you not to think more highly of himself than he ought to think; but to think so as to have sound judgment, as God has allotted to each a measure of faith."* [104] These three elements—gift, authority, and faith—make up our measure of rule, which determines how people will respond to us as servants of God.

You will receive revelation according to your measure of rule. Think of your measure of rule as a stewardship for which you are responsible to God. He will give you revelation in your field of stewardship. If your measure of rule, for example, extends over a small group, look for dreams (and interpretations) that will relate to that small group. Few start out with dreams or revelation that has global ramifications. God may very well give you such a dream, but if He does, it is typically an appetizer or preview for a future time. Before that revelation has application in your life, God will have to enlarge your measure of rule to match it.

Your measure of rule will determine how people respond to you as a servant of God. If you are faithful within your sphere, God will see to it that your gift makes room for you: *"A man's gift makes room for him and brings him before great men."*[105] God never wastes His gifts. If you are faithful with what He has given you, watch out—the sky is the limit!

Categories of Dreams

One fundamental principle of understanding and walking in dream language is learning to distinguish between the two main categories of dreams: *intrinsic* or internal dreams, and *extrinsic* or external dreams. Intrinsic dreams are dreams of self-disclosure. This category encompasses the vast majority of our dreams. Believe it or not, most of your dreams are about you. Most of mine are about me. Most of yours are about you! Never forget, though, that dream language is all about God. Yet He intricately gives us personal dreams of self-disclosure in order to help us in life's journey.

A small percentage of most believers' dreams fall into the extrinsic, or external, category, unless your sphere of influence indicates otherwise. These are dreams of outside events. They may involve you personally but will also have a wider scope. External dreams relate to your *metron* or sphere of influence. Sometimes these dreams will be used to call you to something but not fully release or commission you into it yet either. In this case, think of the dreams as part of your learning curve, your training in your spiritual vocabulary. They are God's teasers to help you get farther down the road. He shows you a glimpse of what lies ahead in order to whet your appetite and inspire you to continue pressing forward. The most common purpose of external dreams is to draw us into intercession.

There are some prophetically gifted people who receive primarily external dreams rather than internal. This usually occurs after God has given them many internal dreams of self-disclosure to cleanse them of the many common-ground issues with the enemy. At the same time, however, God often gives a gift that is larger than our character. Why? To call our character up, to motivate us to greater growth and maturity, and to inspire us to reach for our fullest potential in Christ.

God empowers us with a gift that will cause us to seek Him for the character to carry it.

Dreams From the Holy Spirit

Another fundamental principle for operating in dream language is discerning the sources of our dreams. Essentially, dreams arise from three primary places. There are dreams from the Holy Spirit, dreams from the natural man, and dreams from the demonic realm. We will consider each of these in turn.

Dreams from the Holy Spirit are difficult to categorize because they come in virtually infinite variety and are tailored for each individual. Nevertheless, I want to discuss briefly 12 basic categories of dreams that we receive from the Holy Spirit.

1. Dreams of Destiny

Destiny dreams reveal part of the progressive calling of God regarding your life, guidance, and vocation. Generally, they relate to your sphere of influence. Sometimes they will be extrinsic dreams regarding God's redemptive plan for a city, region, or nation. At times destiny dreams are more personal, revealing the unfolding of your life in God's plan. They may relate only to the present, where you are right now, or they may deal with the past, present, and future of your life. Dream language moves in all three arenas.

A panoramic dream that seems to cover past, present, and future may be fulfilled over a short period of time. On the other hand, many years may pass before your destiny dream is completely fulfilled. This is why it is important to pay close attention to any words you hear in the dream because they will be useful in interpreting the symbols in the dream. Dreams of destiny are inspiring and charge our faith to soar to new levels!

2. Dreams of Edification

These are the "feel good" dreams. When you wake up from them, you absolutely feel great. You feel like you are on top of the world and ready for anything. Edifying dreams are inspirational in tone. They are filled with revelation and they produce hope. If you have been discouraged, you may receive a dream of edification that, even if you do not remember all the details, will instill in you a sense of hope and confidence, thus dispelling your discouragement.

Jacob's dream in the 28th chapter of Genesis is a good example. Fleeing from the wrath of his brother Esau and alone in the wilderness, Jacob was frightened and discouraged. He dreamed of a ladder reaching from earth to Heaven with angels going up and down on it and God standing at the top. God promised to go with Jacob and prosper him. Not only did this dream encourage Jacob, it also changed the course of his life.

In the same way, dreams of edification can help change the course of *your* life.

3. Dreams of Exhortation

Sometimes called "courage dreams," dreams of exhortation often contain a strong sense of urgency. They challenge us to take action. While edification dreams produce hope, exhortational dreams produce faith. They impart inspiration and motivation to get up and do something for Jesus' sake. More than just giving simple advice, dreams of exhortation also reveal an accurate, detailed picture of what is going on behind the scenes, especially in the demonic realm. This revelation is for the purpose of challenging us to take action about what we have seen. Take courage and act!

4. Dreams of Comfort

Comfort dreams serve to heal our emotions and our memories. We can use them to reinterpret circumstances of our past with a heavenly lens, helping us to see things differently. In other words, comfort dreams give us a heavenly perspective on an earthly situation so that we can receive emotional healing.

A few months after my mother passed away, I had a dream where I was back in the old country house where I grew up. I was seated at my old place at the kitchen table, and my mother and father were at opposite ends of the table. Christian singer and songwriter Michael W. Smith were with them, and the three of them sang together Michael's song "Agnus Dei": "Alleluia! Alleluia! For the Lord God Almighty reigns." This dream greatly comforted me and reassured me that my mother, as well as my father, was safely in the presence of the Lord. Muse with me; just sing that sweet song of worship as it is being sung in Heaven!

Thus comfort dreams can also release assurance. If edification dreams produce hope and exhortational dreams release faith, comfort dreams stir up love. They will help you love yourself better, love God better, and love others better as well.

5. Dreams of Correction

Corrective dreams reveal personal changes—character issues, heart issues, repentance issues—that we need to make in order to be able to move forward. These are *not* condemning dreams. The Holy Spirit never condemns. Rather, He comes in gentle love and releases a wooing to draw us to turn to Him and accept His correction. The Holy Spirit convicts and convinces us—but He never condemns.

Unlike a comfort dream, a corrective dream might unsettle us at first. They provoke us and stir us up; they even make us angry sometimes because our natural man does not always want to respond to the things of God. But God, in His infinite patience and loving kindness, relentlessly pursues us. He wants to perfect us, so He sometimes uses dreams of correction.

6. Dreams of Direction

Directive dreams often contain a higher level of revelation and are obviously very prophetic in nature. Quite frequently they will convey a distinct sense of urgency. Their purpose is to give specific guidance, which may even include warnings of some kind. One example is the dream of the wise men in the second chapter of Matthew, whom God warned not to return to Herod. This prompted them to choose an alternate route home.

Sometimes, directive dreams will fill us with a desire for some spiritual quality or dimension that we do not yet possess and inspire us to begin pursuing it. Ultimately, dreams of direction serve to help us get farther down the road toward fulfilling our destiny and purpose, showing us signposts and helping us avoid pitfalls along the way.

7. Dreams of Instruction

These are primarily teaching dreams. Directive dreams give us direction; instructive dreams teach us. There is a fine line of distinction between the two. Scriptures are often highlighted in these dreams, and frequently you will hear a voice speaking to you. Sometimes instructive dreams will even be doctrinal in nature, but they will always contain insight with revelation.

In one dream that I call "A House That is Built to Last," I was at a construction site watching as a cement truck poured layer after layer of concrete into the foundation of a house. Two angels, symbolizing the jealousy of God, stood at the two front corners of the foundation, overseeing the construction. Because of shakings and earthquakes that had occurred over the years, there was a great need for a strong and solid foundation.

As each layer of concrete set, words appeared in the foundation, similar to the handwriting on the wall recorded in the Book of Daniel. At the right front corner of the first layer appeared the words, "Jesus Christ, the Messiah of the Jew and the Gentile." The left corner read, "Apostles and prophets; fathers and mothers of the church ages." The church is built on the foundation of the apostles and prophets, with Christ as the cornerstone.

As the second layer of concrete was poured, the word "Integrity" appeared on the right corner and the word "Humility" on the left. The activity of trucks releasing foundational concrete continued. Across the front of the third layer were the words, "Intimate worship from a pure heart." And, finally, the fourth layer of concrete bore the words, "God's heart for the poor and the desperate." Shooting out from those words was the phrase, "God's healing grace."

I believe that this was an instructive dream with an apostolic nature to it. The dream released teaching insights into the proper way to build a strong house, whether a family home, a business, or a church. All of these qualities are necessary for the proper foundation.

Edifying dreams produce hope. Exhortational dreams instill faith. Comfort dreams stir up love. Instructive dreams impart teaching with wisdom.

8. Dreams of Cleansing

Some people call these "flushing" dreams, and with good reason. One of the most common images associated with the cleansing dream is that of being in the bathroom, on the toilet or taking a shower. These dreams deal with cleansing issues. To use scriptural terminology, we could call these dreams of sanctification. They are concerned with our purification process.

Cleansing dreams are used to wash us from the dust and dirt that we pick up by walking in the world. Christ is preparing a Bride in whom will be no spot or wrinkle, not even on our garments. Sometimes our hearts and minds become tainted by our contact with the sin and evil in the world. Vile corruption attempts to put its grim on us. Sanctifying dreams can help with that process. Essentially, these dreams are all about applying the cleansing blood of Jesus to our lives.

9. Dreams Revealing the Heart

These are also known as dreams of self-disclosure or dreams of self-condition. Scripture says, *"The heart is more deceitful than all else and is desperately sick; who can understand it?"*[106] And Jesus said, *"For out of the abundance of the heart the mouth speaks."*[107] Self-disclosure dreams show us where we presently stand with God. For example, let's say that you dream that you are in your car and stuck in a cul-de-sac. The car may represent your life or your ministry, and the cul-de-sac reveals that you are going around in circles or have almost reached a dead end. God doesn't want you to be at a dead end; He wants you back out on the highway of life.

When Abimelech took Abraham's wife, Sarah, into his harem, thinking she was Abraham's sister (which is what Abraham had told him), God appeared to Abimelech in a dream and warned him not to go any farther because Sarah was Abraham's wife. God told Abimelech to restore Sarah to Abraham or else he would die. The king did as he was instructed in the dream.[108]

God gives us dreams of self-condition to show us where we are, tell us what we need to do, and reveal where He wants us to go.

10. Dreams of Spiritual Warfare

Spiritual warfare dreams are calls to prayer. They are intercessory-type dreams that reveal hindrances that are in the way and may include calls to worship and fasting. Their purpose is to inspire us to press through to victory to the cross of Christ, tearing down strongholds and overcoming every obstacle or barrier that stands in the way.

Sometimes dreams come in pairs and carry the same meaning to give additional insight. Recently, when I was diagnosed with a recurrence of non-Hodgkin's Lymphoma cancer, the Lord gave me two dreams that encouraged me to fight on to victory. In the first dream, the Holy Spirit said to me, "You must call forth a courtroom hearing and bring before the judge three generational spirits: generational infirmity, generational witchcraft, and a generational thievery."

In the second dream I was handed a revolver with a chamber for holding five rounds. Then I was handed five bullets of "effective grace" for loading the revolver. Each bullet had a Scripture reference on it:

1. Jeremiah 30:17: "'*For I will restore you to health and I will heal you of your wounds,' declares the Lord....*"

2. Proverbs 6:30-31: "*Men do not despise a thief if he steals to satisfy himself when he is hungry; but when he is found, he must repay sevenfold; he must give all the substance of his house.*"

3. Leviticus 17:11: "*For the life of the flesh is in the blood....*"

4. Isaiah 54:17: "*No weapon that is formed against you will prosper; and every tongue that accuses you in judgment you will condemn....*"

5. Matthew 8:16-17: "*When evening came, they brought to Him many who were demon-possessed; and He cast out the spirits with a word, and healed all who were ill. This was to fulfill what was spoken through Isaiah the prophet: 'He Himself took our infirmities and carried away our diseases.'*"

I believe the Lord gave me these Scriptures through a spiritual warfare dream to arm me to be effective in the battle. I sent this dream out to our prayer shield and asked them to proclaim these five Scriptures over my life.

11. Dreams of Creativity

Creative dreams involve such things as designs, inventions, and new ways of doing things. They can charge our spirit man and help us become change makers, changing the culture of our homes, cities, and the lives of others and even the strongholds of our minds. God often uses creative dreams with artistic people to give them songs to sing, pictures to paint, or words to write. I have had dreams revealing the title of a new book along with a brilliant artistic cover. I call these "Holy Ghost cheat sheets" and I can use all of them He wants to give!

Some years ago I was preparing to go to Ohio for a week of ministry. It was the height of the early prophetic movement, and the unusual amount of prophetic activity that was going on had raised expectations enormously high. Frankly, I had been moving in a level of revelation that was new to me at that time, and I was afraid that people were going to expect me to move at that level all the time. Pressure. Performance. Fear. As the day for my departure drew nearer, I was struggling with anxiety. I cried to the Lord for help, and He heard me!

The night before I left, I received two dreams or, rather, the same dream twice. An orchestra was playing, and a choir was singing. A banner unfurled in front of my eyes. Written on the banner were the words to a song. I realized that the orchestra was playing the melody and the choir was singing those words. That is when I woke up. Twice this occurred.

I flew to Cleveland, Ohio, and all that week, in every church sanctuary I ministered in, I searched for that banner. I really wanted to find that banner. I just knew it would be somewhere! I kept looking in the natural everywhere I went! The reason: I forgot the words that were printed on it! I kept looking for this sign from God, but place after place, it evaded me.

On the last night of the meetings I had a vision of a pair of shoes that I would be given to symbolically wear. On several occasions I have had visions of the shoes of an apostolic or prophetic leader as a clue to me of what particular anointing I was about to move in. This night I saw the shoes of my dear friend Mahesh Chavda. Having traveled with Mahesh and witnessed his meetings, I knew that in my last meeting the Holy Spirit would move in power and people would be overwhelmed by the Holy Spirit all over the auditorium.

By the time of the last night's meeting, however, I was so physically depleted that I felt like I had nothing left to give to the people. When the time came for me to speak, I was introduced, but I still seemed to have nothing. Desperately I prayed, "Help me, Jesus!"

God is so faithful! As I stood up to speak, I received an open vision of—you guessed it—the unfurled banner from my dream. There it was, right in front of my spiritual eyes. I could see clearly the words written on it and immediately began to sing them a cappella: "How far will My love extend? How far will My arm reach? Will My blood cleanse when man sins, yet knowing? How far will the blood of My Son reach?"

As it turned out, this was a song of great comfort to this church, as they recently had removed a senior leader who had fallen into immorality and were currently without a permanent leader. They were dealing with a lot of disappointment, and the song of the Lord greatly encouraged them. God knew just what they needed and imparted it to me through a creative dream and vision. That night the anointing was so strong that no one could come closer than six feet from me without falling out in the Spirit. People were dropping by the power of God all over the sanctuary.

Was this a dream of comfort, dream of cleansing, or dream of creativity? Well, remember the illustration I shared previously about the colors of the rainbow? Where one color ends the other begins? Well, the answer is: it was all the above. It was a creative dream that brought cleansing and healing comfort! Dreams can do more than one thing at a time!

God is a Creator by nature, and He loves to give creative dreams to His children.

12. Dreams With Impartation

Impartational dreams are used to activate any of the various dimensions of the gifts of the Spirit. Many times it will be the gift of healing, both emotional healing and physical healing. In some cases an angel of the Lord may actually appear in your room and touch you, releasing one of Heaven's many power encounters.

My wife, Michal Ann, had a dream like this two weeks before she was scheduled to go to Mozambique. A number of people had been telling her that she was not well enough to go on this trip. In her dream, Aimee Semple McPherson, the apostle, evangelist, and founder of the Four Square Gospel church who moved mightily in signs and wonders, approached Michal Ann with a key card in her hand. She stuck it into her and pulled it back out. Upon awakening, Michal Ann felt the riveting presence of the energy of God all over her. It was a dream of impartation. There was an impartation of faith not only for her own life but for the entire apostolic mission she was about to embark upon leading a team to Mozambique. Yes, God knows exactly what you need and when you need it!

Dreams From the Natural Man

Some of our dreams are not supernatural in nature but come from our natural man. These "natural" dreams generally fall into one of three categories: body dreams, chemical dreams, or soulish dreams.

1. Body Dreams

Body dreams generally arise from and reflect some aspect of the physical condition of the person who is dreaming. For example, dreams of being pregnant are not uncommon. They often mean—you got it—the lady is pregnant! But even men have been known to have dreams of being pregnant. In their case, as well as in the case of women who dream they are pregnant but are not, there may indeed be a spiritual meaning behind the dream. A pregnancy dream may indicate that the person is "due" with the things and purposes of God. Something new is about to be birthed!

Most often, however, body dreams reflect physical realities. A person who is sick may dream of being sick. A person feeling like they have the flu, well, they might have the flu! A person who is experiencing depression or grief may have dreams that reflect their state of mind. Somber and depressing dreams can also come from the enemy, so careful discernment is called for in distinguishing one from the other.

Just because body dreams are not necessarily spiritual does not mean that they are demonic. It is important to pay attention to body dreams because they can provide clues to changes we may need to make in our natural life.

2. Chemical Dreams

These dreams, sometimes known as hormone dreams, usually come as a result of medications we are taking. Quite often, chemical dreams reveal the need for our bodies to go through some cleansing. I have had occasions when a chemical dream revealed to me that a medication I was taking, such as for sinus relief, was building up in my body too much. It was having a negative effect on me, and I needed cleansing.

Chemical dreams may also arise because of changing or abnormal hormone or chemical levels in the body. PMS, diabetes, hypoglycemia—these and similar conditions involving chemical imbalances can stimulate these type of natural dreams.

3. Soulish Dreams

The word "soulish" does not necessarily mean fleshly. As Christians, our souls are to be renewed in Christ—but honestly, we are all in various stages of being renewed. Soulish dreams may simply be our emotions expressing our needs or desires. They may speak to us about the need for sanctification in some area of our life. One significant value of soulish dreams is that they can show us things about ourselves that we may otherwise fail to see when awake.

Dreams From the Demonic Realm

A third source of dreams that we must recognize is that of the demonic realm. Anything that God has and uses, the enemy seeks to counterfeit, including dreams. Demonic dreams tend to fall into any of three different types: dark dreams, dreams of fear and/or panic, and dreams of deception.

1. Dark Dreams

Dark dreams tend to be dark in two ways. First, they are dark in mood and tone: somber, depressing, melancholy dreams; dreams where everything is a little out of kilter, where something indefinable seems wrong or slightly off center. Second, dark dreams typically are literally dark with subdued or muted colors. Black, gray, and sickly green shades are in abundance. This lack of bright, vivid, and lively colors is one way of determining that a dream may come from a dark or even demonic source.

Dark dreams commonly conjure up dark emotions and often employ dark symbols, emblems that instill a sense of discomfort or unease. This is the type of dream that I referred to in the second chapter. Remember, I had a fair number of dark dreams before I was ever released into cleansing and later the power of extrinsic dreams. Of course, there are also dark chemical dreams that are brought on as a result of involvement with witchcraft and illegal drug use. Repent, turn to the Lord, and seek help if this is the case.

2. Dreams of Fear and/or Panic

Most nightmares, especially childhood nightmares, fall into this category. Dreams of fear and panic often arise from trauma, so simply rebuking the fear or the panic may not be enough. It may be necessary to ask the Holy Spirit to reveal the root of the frightening dreams so that repentance, cleansing, or healing can take place. My wife's early dreams of bears and tornadoes were ones of this nature. Learn to exercise your authority in Christ and ward off these haunting dreams in Jesus' name!

3. Dreams of Deception

Deceptive dreams are often the work of deceitful spirits, which Scripture says will be particularly active in the last days: *"But the Spirit explicitly says that in later times some will fall away from the faith, paying attention to deceitful spirits and doctrines of demons."*[109] These deceptive spirits seek to draw us away from the place of security to a place of insecurity.

The purpose of deceptive dreams is to create images and impressions in our minds that will turn us away from the true path of God's light into the darkness of error and heresy. Under the influence of deceptive dreams we can make mistakes in every area of life: doctrine, finances, sexuality, relationships, career choices, parenting; you name it. Whatever form they may take and whatever images they may convey, these disturbing revelations are from the dark side. Exercise careful discernment. Walking in the light of transparent relationships with other believers in the Body of Christ is ammunition that overcomes the deceptive spirit.

Keeping It Simple

In case you are starting to worry about information overload with all these categories of dreams, let me close by breaking all this down into simpler terms. According to authors Chuck Pierce and Rebecca Sytsema, all these categories we have discussed can be condensed into three basic dream types: the simple message dream, the simple symbolic dream, and the complex symbolic dream. In their book *When God Speaks*, Chuck Pierce and Rebecca Sytsema explain it this way:

We find three types of dreams in the Bible:

1. **A simple message dream.** In Matthew 1–2, Joseph understood the dreams concerning Mary and Herod. There was no real need for interpretation. These dreams were direct, to the point, and self-interpreted.

2. **A simple symbolic dream.** Dreams can be filled with symbols. Oftentimes the symbolism is clear enough that the dreamer and others can understand it without any complicated interpretation. For instance, when Joseph had his dream in Genesis 37, he fully understood it, as did his brothers, to the point that they wanted to kill him, even though it had symbols of the sun, moon, and stars.

3. **The complex symbolic dream.** This type of dream needs interpretative skill from someone who has unusual ability in the gift of interpretation or from someone who knows how to seek God to find revelation. We find this type of dream in the life of Joseph, when he interprets Pharaoh's dream. In Daniel 2 and 4, we find good examples of this type of dream. In Daniel 8, we find a dream in which Daniel actually sought divine interpretation.[110]

If you are just beginning to walk in the realm of dream language and find this great diversity of dreams a bit overwhelming, be patient. It will take time and experience to become adept at identifying different dream types and categories and interpreting the messages you receive. Relax in the assurance that God will not move you along faster than you can handle. He will gently and lovingly guide you along the way in your very own diversity of dreams.

Yes, dream a little dream with me. His ways are amazing. He will lead you not only into revelation but He will teach you how to understand what you just received!

Reflection Questions

1. What does it mean that we each receive diverse dreams that are according to our sphere? How does this relate to you?

2. Twelve categories of dreams we receive from the Holy Spirit are discussed. Name three of these that seem to be ones that you have experienced.

3. What are the three types of dreams that come from the demonic side? What are some of their characteristics?

Referral Reading

Chuck Pierce, *When God Speaks* (Ventura, CA: Regal Books, 2005).

James W. Goll, *Experiencing Dreams and Vision Study Guide* (Franklin, TN: Encounters Network, 2005).

► ► ► ► ► ►
► ► ► ► ► ►
► ► ► ► ► ►
► ► ► ► ► ►
► ► ► ► ► ►
► ► ► ► ► ►
► ► ► ► ► ►

CHAPTER SEVEN

UNDERSTANDING THE DREAMS YOU DREAM

Does understanding and interpreting dreams seem to you like a giant maze with no apparent end in sight? If so, take comfort! Others throughout the ages have felt the same way! But the Lord, the Master Dream Weaver, has a word of encouragement for you (and for all of us): "I will be your Helper!"

God loves to help the helpless. And, when it comes to spiritual matters, we are all helpless without Him. Without the grace, love, and mercy of God there would be no repentance, no forgiveness, no salvation, and no revelation. We would be lost and completely without hope. God knows we are helpless. That is why He sent His Son Jesus to die on the cross for our sins, and why He sent the Holy Spirit to abide in the heart of every believer. The Spirit will guide us into all the truth and into all the things of God. The Gospel of John affirms this over and over:

I will ask the Father, and He will give you another Helper, that He may be with you forever; that is the Spirit of truth, whom the world cannot receive, because it does not see Him or know Him, but you know Him because He abides with you and will be in you. [111]

But the Helper, the Holy Spirit, whom the Father will send in My name, He will teach you all things, and bring to your remembrance all that I said to you. [112]

When the Helper comes, whom I will send to you from the Father, that is the Spirit of truth who proceeds from the Father, He will testify about Me. [113]

But I tell you the truth, it is to your advantage that I go away; for if I do not go away, the Helper will not come to you; but if I go, I will send Him to you. [114]

Because the Holy Spirit lives inside of us, we each have our own personal Tutor in the ways and the mind and the heart of God:

But when He, the Spirit of truth, comes, He will guide you into all the truth; for He will not speak on His own initiative, but whatever He hears, He will speak; and He will disclose to you what is to come. He will glorify Me, for He will take of Mine and will disclose it to you. All things that the Father has are Mine; therefore I said that He takes of Mine and will disclose it to you. [115]

I have had many wonderful teachers and mentors through the years—precious people every one—but none can match the Holy Spirit Himself. He is also my personal friend. He is with me wherever I go. He speaks the wisdom ways of God to me and opens the Word of God to my understanding. He convicts me of sin yet loves me deeply. He always speaks the truth to me, and He never gives up.

In my book, *The Beginner's Guide to Hearing God,* I wrote:

The Holy Spirit is our counselor and our teacher, yet He is more than a teacher—more like a tutor. But He is not just any tutor; He's the kind who truly loves to spend individual, personal time with each of His students. He is like that rare kind of guidance counselor who actually becomes a friend. He is like the teacher who becomes a personal mentor. ...As a personal Tutor, He is also a personal coach to help us win out on the playing field of life.

In addition—great news!—He's not like an ordinary tutor or teacher who clocks in and out. As we graduate from one level of spiritual development to the next, He remains our lifelong personal Tutor. We start with the best and we end with the best. As we end our days here on Earth, He even prepares us for our postgraduate course in life hereafter! All along, He individually instructs us as to what life lessons we need to learn, and even in what order to take them.[116]

The Holy Spirit is our Guide through the maze of dream types and categories, and He is our Instructor in dream language. Since He is always with us, He is available all the time, at any time day or night. When we have questions or need wisdom or knowledge, all we have to do is ask. James said, "*You do not have because you do not ask,*"[117] and, "*But if any of you lacks wisdom, let him ask of God, who gives to all generously and without reproach, and it will be given to him.*"[118] This echoes Jesus' own words, "*For everyone who asks receives, and he who seeks finds, and to him who knocks it will be opened.*"[119]

In the discussion that follows, we will trust the Holy Spirit to give us illumination as we examine some of the most common dreams that people experience and seek to understand the meanings behind common dream elements.

"Holy Spirit, we stand ready to learn and eager to understand. Please teach us!"

The Twenty Most Common Dreams

Various ministries and organizations have logged literally thousands of dreams and therefore have been able to decipher the most common dreams that people have. The following is a partial listing of these most common types of dreams. This list is not comprehensive, and the dreams are not listed in any particular order. In other words, they are not ranked by most common to least common or by any other ranking factor.

1. Dreams of Your House

This one would easily rank in the top five most common dreams. Virtually all of us have had one or more dreams in which our house appears, either the house we currently live in or one where we once lived in the past. The house normally represents your life, and the circumstances taking place in the house reflect the specific activities in your life. These dreams may also represent a church as well.

Individual rooms of the house may represent specific things. For instance, if the bedroom appears, the dream may have something to do with issues of intimacy. The bathroom may represent a need for cleansing. The family room may be a clue that God wants to work on family relationships, either your nuclear family or your church family. This is one of the most common dreams that my wife has had over the years.

2. Dreams of Going to School

These dreams often center on the taking of tests. The tests may be for the purpose of promotion. Or you might find yourself searching for your next class—an indication that guidance is needed or a graduation has just occurred. You might be repeating a class you took before, possibly meaning that you have an opportunity to learn from past failures. High school dreams may be a sign that you are enrolled in the School of the Holy Spirit (H.S.=High School=Holy Spirit). There are limitless possibilities. These are just a few examples. Interesting enough, the Teacher is always silent when giving a test!

3. Dreams of Various Vehicles

These may indicate the calling you have on your life, the vehicle of purpose that will carry you from one point to another. Cars, planes, buses, etc., may be symbols of the type or even the size of the ministry you are or will be engaged in. That's why there are different kinds of vehicles. Note the color of the vehicle. If it is a car, what is the make and model? Observe who is driving it. Are you driving or is someone else driving? If someone else is driving, who is it? Do you know the person? Is it a person from your past? If the driver is faceless, this may refer to a person who will appear sometime in your future or that the Holy Spirit Himself is your driving guide.

4. Dreams Concerning Storms

Storm dreams tend to be intercessory, spiritual warfare-type dreams. They are particularly common for people who have a calling or gift in the area of the discerning of spirits. These dreams often hint of things that are on the horizon—both dark, negative storms of demonic attack for the purpose of prayer, intercession, and spiritual warfare, as well as showers of blessing that are imminent.

5. Dreams of Flying or Soaring

Flying dreams deal with your spiritual capacity to rise above problems and difficulties and to soar into the heavenlies. These are some of the most inspirational and encouraging in tone of all dreams. When awakening from a dream where you fly or soar, you often wake up feeling exhilarated—even inebriated—in the Spirit. Ascending-type dreams are more unusual yet edifying. Remember, we are seated with Christ Jesus in the heavenly places far above all principalities and powers.

6. *Dreams of Being Naked or Exposed*

These dreams indicate that you will be or are becoming transparent and vulnerable. Depending on your particular situation, this may be exhilarating or fearful and could reveal feelings of shame. Note: these dreams are not meant to produce embarrassment but rather draw you into greater intimacy with the Lord and indicate places where greater transparency is required. These types of dreams often appear during times of transition where you are being dismantled in order to be re-mantled.

7. *Dreams of the Condition of Your Teeth*

Often, these dreams reveal the need for wisdom. Are your teeth loose, rotten, falling out, or are they bright and shiny? Do you have a good bite? Are you able to chew your cud? Teeth represent wisdom, and often teeth appear loose in a dream. What does that mean? It may mean that you need a wisdom application for something you are about to bite off. The fear of the Lord is the beginning of wisdom.

8. *Dreams of Past Relationships*

This kind of dream may indicate that you are being tempted to fall back into old patterns and ways of thinking. Depending upon who the person is in the dream, and what this person represents to you, these dreams might also be an indication of your need to renew your former desires and godly passions for good things in life.

Seeing a person from your past does not usually mean that you will literally renew your old relationship with that individual. Look more for what that person represents in your life—for good or bad. A person who was bad in your life may represent God's warning to you not to relapse into old habits and mind-sets that were not profitable. On the other hand, a person who was good in your life may represent God's desire or intention to restore good times that you thought were gone.

9. *Dreams of Dying*

These dreams are not normally about the person seen in the dream in a literal sense, but are symbolic about something that is passing away or departing from your life. The type of death may be important to note. Watch, though, to see if resurrection is on the other side.

Not long ago I had a dream where I was observing my own funeral. Because I was battling cancer at the time, this dream really shook me up for a while until the Lord showed me what it really meant. I was back in my hometown in Missouri, driving a white pickup truck. My mom and dad, who are both in Heaven, were in the truck with me. I drove by our old Methodist church and saw a white hearse outside. I watched as pallbearers dressed in black brought a white casket out of the church and placed it into the hearse. Upon awakening, I realized that I was watching my own funeral.

The dream was in black and white rather than color, which was a clue to its true meaning. God was tipping me off to the enemy's desire to place a spirit of death in my thoughts. The Lord was actually strengthening me to stand against this disease as well as the spirit of death behind it. Wage war with the dreams of insight that the Lord gives to you. Fight the enemy's plans in Jesus' name!

10. Dreams of Birth

Normally these dreams are not about an actual childbirth but rather about new seasons of purpose and destiny coming forth into your life. If a name is given to the child, pay close attention because that usually indicates that a new season in the purposes of God is being birthed. While I say this, there are exceptions. I remember so fondly, when my wife was pregnant with our third child, Tyler Hamilton, that she had a dream that she gave birth to a little girl named Rachel. I told her that was a symbolic dream. But true to form, she was right and I was wrong—child number four came along, and her name, of course, is Rachel!

11. Dreams of Taking a Shower

These are cleansing-type dreams (toilets, showers, bathtubs, etc.) revealing things that are in the process of being flushed out of your life, cleansed and flushed away. These are good dreams by the way. Enjoy the showers of God's love and mercy and get cleansed from the dirt of the world and its ways. Apply the blood of Jesus and get ready for a new day!

12. Dreams of Falling

These dreams may reveal a fear you have of losing control of some area of your life or, on the positive side, that you are actually becoming free of directing your own life. What substance you fall into in the dream is a major key to proper understanding. The outstanding primary emotions in these dreams will indicate which way to interpret them. Falling can be fearful, but it can also represent falling into the ocean of God's love.

13. Dreams of Chasing and Being Chased

Chasing dreams often reveal enemies that are at work, coming against your life and purpose. On the opposite side, they may indicate the passionate pursuit of God in your life, and you towards Him. Are you being chased? By whom? What emotions do you feel? Are you afraid of getting caught? Or maybe you are the one doing the chasing. Who are you chasing? Why? Again, what emotions do you feel during the chase? The answers to these questions and, particularly, the dominant emotions in the dream, will often help determine the direction of its interpretation. Often the Lord appears in various forms, motioning to us, saying, "Catch Me if you can!"

14. Dreams of Relatives, Alive and Dead

Most likely, these dreams indicate generational issues at work in your life—both blessings and curses. You will need discernment as to whether to accept the blessing or cut off the darkness. This is particularly true if grandparents appear in your dreams, as they will typically indicate generational issues.

One night I had a dream in which I saw my grandfather standing on the porch of his old country house, dressed in his overalls. His white hair was shining, and he had an incredible smile on his face. To this day I am still pondering over the full meaning of this dream. My grandfather may have been a symbol for God the Father, the Ancient of Days, appearing on the front porch of our family house drawing us unto Himself.

15. Dreams Called Nightmares

Nightmares tend to be more frequent with children and new believers in Christ, just as calling dreams do. They may reveal generational enemies at work that need to be cut off. Stand against the enemies of fear. Call forth the opposite presence of the amazing love of God, which casts out fear, for fear has torment!

16. Dreams of Snakes

The snake dream is probably one of the most common of all the categories of animal dreams. These dreams reveal the serpent—the devil with his demonic hosts—at work through accusation, lying, attacks, etc. Other common dreams of this nature include dreams of spiders, bears, and even alligators. Spiders and bears are the two other major animals that appear in dreams that show fear. The spider in particular, releasing its deadly poison, is often a symbol of witchcraft and the occult.

17. Dreams of Dogs and Cats

After snakes, the most common animal to appear in dreams is the dog. A dog in your dream usually indicates friendship, loyalty, protection, and good feelings. On the other hand, dog dreams may also reveal the dark side, including growling, attacking, biting, etc. Sometimes these dreams reveal a friend who is about to betray you.

Dreams with cats are also quite common. These dreams also vary in nature with everything from the feeling of being loved, to being smothered, to persnickety attitudes, the occult, and even witchcraft.

18. Dreams of Going Through Doors

These dreams generally reveal change that is coming. New ways, new opportunities, and new advancements are on the way. Similar to dreams of doors are dreams including elevators or escalators, which indicate that you are rising higher into your purpose and your calling.

19. Dreams of Clocks and Watches

Clocks or watches in a dream reveal what time it is in your life, or the need for a wake-up call in the Body of Christ or in a nation. It is time to be alert and watchful. These dreams may indicate a Scripture verse as well, giving a deeper message. Are you a watchman on the walls? If so, what watch are you on?

20. Dreams With Scripture Verses

Sometimes you may have a dream in which Bible passages appear, indicating a message from God. This phenomenon may occur in a number of ways: verbal quotes where you actually hear a voice quoting the passage, digital clock-type readouts, and dramatizations of a scene from the Bible, just to name a few. Quite often these are watchmen-type dreams, dreams of instructions filled with the ways of wisdom.

Michal Ann had a dream of this type. Her Bible was open and filled with all kinds of notes. Somewhere, somehow, she picked up on the number 111 but did not understand what it meant. When she woke up all she knew was that it somehow referred to Scripture. She searched her Bible for a little while but could not find the right passage. After asking the Holy Spirit for guidance, she fell asleep again and had a second dream. In this second dream, Mike Bickle, leader of the International House of Prayer in Kansas City, came up to her with his Bible open and said, "It is Colossians 1:11." Upon waking the second time, Michal Ann looked up the Scripture: "[We pray] *that you may be invigorated and strengthened with all power, according to the might of His glory,* [to exercise] *every kind of endurance and patience* (perseverance and forbearance) *with joy*."[120] That verse has become a life message for Michal Ann. Why? She needed that word in her own life, and today the Lord uses her to give that word away, imparting it to release that nature of God in others.

People Who Appear in Your Dreams

Another extremely common occurrence in dreams is the appearance of people: family members, friends, acquaintances, prominent leaders in church, society, or government and even complete strangers. In the majority of these cases, the people who appear in your dreams are symbolic in nature. Seeing a person in a dream does not necessarily mean that you will have an encounter with that person.

There are three basic questions you can ask to help you interpret dreams in which certain people appear:

1. Who is this person in relation to you?

2. What does this person's name mean?

3. What character trait or calling does this person represent to you?

Although no list of people who appear in our dreams could ever be comprehensive, the list that follows cites the most common people or type of people that you are likely to encounter in your dreams, along with their probable symbolism.

1. A man or woman of God in your life most probably represents a particular type of message being delivered. The important issue here is not who the person is but the message he or she bears. Focus in on the message. That is where you will most likely find the meaning behind the dream.

2. An untrustworthy person in your past may indicate a coming situation that you should not trust. Seeing someone in a dream from your past that is associated with a betrayal or a bad situation may be a warning from the Holy Spirit. These may be calls to prayer to cut off a bad situation.

3. A healing evangelist (prophetic person, etc.) appearing in your dream usually represents a healing grace that is coming your way. The identity of that healing evangelist or prophetic person is not as important as what he or she represents—the kind of ministry associated with that person.

4. A husband in your dream often means that Christ Jesus the Lord is drawing ever so close in a covenant relationship.

5. Getting married in a dream usually relates to growing intimacy with God or a new joining that is coming your way. Keep in mind, opposites attract.

6. Dreams with dead people in them speak of the common sentiment attached to those deceased loved ones. This is *not* an indication that you are "crossing over" or actually visiting this person from your past in order to receive guidance! Do not equate this with the error of seeking guidance from the spirits of the dead, as King Saul did with the spirit of Samuel.[121] God is simply giving you a snapshot of something that the dead person represents.

7. Dreams of presidents and other people in authority are often calls to pray for national events. I used to have dreams of President Clinton where he and I were walking together and I would take his hand and suddenly be able to feel the condition of his heart. And then I would pray for him, interceding not

only for his heart's condition but also for the burden or challenges of our nation.

8. A faceless person often appears in dreams as an indication of the presence of the Holy Spirit, or possibly even angels, in your life. Sometimes people dream of a faceless man driving a bus but they don't know who he is. This too often represents the Holy Spirit, driving the bus of your life and steering you into your life mission.

R-rated Dreams—Am I Sick or What?

One aspect of dreaming that many people are embarrassed to talk about, much less admit to, is the aspect of dreams that contain sexual content and/or nudity. This is an important point as many people worry that if they have such occasional dreams it automatically means they have a dirty mind, a moral problem, or some such thing. Often, however, dreams with sexual content have nothing to do literally with sexual intercourse.

The difficulty with dealing with "R-rated" dreams is illustrated by the fact that several different schools of thought exist regarding these dreams and how they should be interpreted. Generally, there are four of these. Depending on one's point of view, sexually charged dreams are:

A spiritual call to greater intimacy.

A warning of one's need of cleansing of attitudes of the mind, motives of the heart, and/or even acts of immorality.

A calling or a joining of union with another person or even people group.

Natural body dreams containing the biological and physical desires that are common to most people.

In actuality, sexual dreams cannot be confined to just any one of these four categories alone. All of them are valid at one time or another depending on the specific dream. When dealing with this kind of dream, allow for the possibility of it authentically being a body dream. It is not necessary always to spiritualize everything. Sometimes there is no spiritual content. Sometimes a dream is just a dream.

To aid you in understanding and interpreting dreams with sexual content, here are some important questions to consider:

1. Is it the same sex? Is it the opposite sex? Don't take the images at face value, particularly if same-gender sex is involved. Look for a higher meaning. For example, much of the church world breeds only after its own kind; we tend to only relate to those who are most like us. The dream may indicate a need to cross-pollinate with other members of the Body of Christ. Spiritual "inbreeding" leads to weakness and eventual extinction. Multiplication comes from sowing your seed into those who are opposite of you.

2. Is it an old love or a new love? This could indicate what you currently are passionate about. Are you being tempted to go back to something old? Is there something new on the horizon that you are becoming passionate about?

3. Does this person seem to take the place of the Lord? If so, there is a serious need for cleansing and dealing with issues of idolatry.

4. Does the dream leave you feeling dirty or clean? A dirty feeling probably means that cleansing and/or repentance of some kind are needed. Feeling clean usually points to a more positive interpretation.

5. Are you or others naked in the dream? Transparency is a good thing. But often in these dreams everyone can see what is going on in your life. These dreams are not to embarrass you but to encourage you in your vulnerability with others.

Sexual Dreams—Carnal or Spiritual?

For additional insight into this troubling area of discerning sexual dreams, I want to share with you a few thoughts from two respected authors and leaders who are experienced authorities on understanding and interpreting dreams. The first is Joy Parrott, a wonderful, godly lady who is a wife and a mother as well as a prophetic intercessor and teacher. In her book, *Parables in the Night Seasons*, she relates a personal sexual dream that illustrates the challenge of understanding and interpreting this kind of dream:

I can remember the first dream I had which seemed totally out of character for me. The dream came even after I had been applying the truths from chapter four and had already received much healing on major issues. I woke from this dream and wondered just what it could have meant. This dream began with me walking home after being seen by a doctor who had told me that I was pregnant. I was pondering how I was going to tell my husband this information, especially since I knew that the baby was not his. In my mind I didn't know how this had happened. I knew that even if I had wanted to, I could not pass this child off as my husband's, because this child's father was from a different nationality. How could I tell my husband this news? What would he do? Upon entering the house, I told him that I had some news and he replied that he already knew. I was shocked that he had known, but exclaimed that I didn't know how it happened—I never did anything! I was defending myself because I didn't know how this happened. But my husband had a come back to my every word. He believed the report of the pregnancy and couldn't believe in my innocence. When I awoke my pounding heart was nearly in my throat. I wondered what this dream was all about. My immediate thoughts were that I had misunderstood somehow the things that God had taught me about dreams and reckoned within myself that Satan had given me this dream. I knew that I had never done anything like this dream suggested, and believe that I never would. Once I chalked this dream up to Satan, I thought it would go away, but it wouldn't leave me. God finally gave the interpretation of this dream to me, but only after I'd suffered for what seemed like an eternity, yet had only been a few hours. God said to me, "You indeed are pregnant and this child is not of the same race because you are pregnant with ministry that the Holy Spirit has given you and you will not be able to pass this off as being your husband's because this is Mine!" Wow! How tremendous! And to think that I had blamed the whole dream on Satan! Now any person would have thought this dream to have been from the enemy or at least our old carnal nature. But the dream was from God! Not everything that appears to be carnal is from our soul. I have awakened many times sweating and concerned over what I had just seen or experienced in a dream. (With such dreams, I am always glad to find out that I was only dreaming!)[122]

Even such an experienced dream journeyer as Joy Parrott was unable to correctly interpret her sexual dream until God revealed its meaning to her.

Dr. Joe Ibojie provides a slightly different slant in his book, *Dreams and Visions*:

Sex in a dream suggests that you are probably making, or about to make, decisions based on a carnal nature. In Scripture, God frequently uses sexual immorality as an allegory for unfaithfulness, or deviation from spiritual truth. Frequent experience of sex in dreams speaks of carnality, but it also indicates a hidden, unbroken stronghold of lust. Rape indicates violation of the dreamer's person or integrity, and this must be averted in prayer. [123]

To further clarify the different ways that sexual dreams can be interpreted, here are some final thoughts from Joy Parrott:

God is not a prude and He may give you some dreams that will have you sure they couldn't be from Him, yet they are. Of course, many of these will not be divine, especially if we continue to walk in the things of this world and satisfy our fleshly desires. Yet God has recorded some risqué things in the scripture which confirms that He is not a prude. In the book of Ezekiel, God refers to Jerusalem, His people, as harlots! In Hosea, God tells the prophet Hosea to marry a prostitute as a prophetic drama of His unconditional love for His people. God told Isaiah to run around naked for three years prophesying to everything in sight! …Such examples show that God isn't concerned about offending us or sparing our "holy ears" from hearing such things. God wants to speak to us and sometimes He will get downright blunt! He is going to speak in a language that we will understand. [124]

Understanding our dreams is one thing; interpreting them is another. The next chapter will examine dream interpretation in detail. In closing, however, let me leave you with a biblical promise and a thought related to understanding our dreams:

Call to Me and I will answer you, and I will tell you great and mighty things, which you do not know. [125]

Dreams do not explain the future—the future will explain the dreams.

Reflection Questions

1. In gaining understanding of the dreams we dream, what is the role of the Holy Spirit?

2. This chapter lists 20 of the most common dreams along with short descriptions. What are five of the most common dreams people have?

3. There are four possible ways of interpreting dreams with sexual content. What are they?

Referral Reading

Joy Parrott, *Parables in the Night Season* (Renton, WA: Glory Publications, 2002).

Jim W. Goll, *The Beginner's Guide to Hearing God* (Ventura, CA: Regal Books, 2004).

Dr. Joe Obojie, *Dreams and Visions* (Pescara, Italy: Destiny Image Europe, 2005).

▶ ▶ ▶ ▶ ▶ ▶
▶ ▶ ▶ ▶ ▶ ▶
▶ ▶ ▶ ▶ ▶ ▶
▶ ▶ ▶ ▶ ▶ ▶
▶ ▶ ▶ ▶ ▶ ▶
▶ ▶ ▶ ▶ ▶ ▶
▶ ▶ ▶ ▶ ▶ ▶

CHAPTER EIGHT

PROPERLY
INTERPRETING
DREAMS

Some years ago I was traveling through the night by train from the Frankfurt, Germany, region to Rossenheim in southern Bavaria. I was in one of the sleeping cars but, unable to sleep, I spent much of my time praying in the Spirit. The Holy Spirit kept speaking to me over and over, "Where are My Daniels? Where are My Esthers? Where are My Josephs, and where are My Deborahs?"

After many years of pondering on this word, I believe that the Holy Spirit is on a quest to find believers He can work with—believers who will dream God's dreams at any cost, have a discerning spirit to properly interpret the times, and who learn to intercede out of a posture of revelation.

Daniel, Esther, Joseph, and Deborah were godly people who possessed the spirit of revelation and who altered destinies and changed history through the revelation that was bestowed on them. They trusted the Lord for wisdom and insight and served His purposes in their generation. Today the Spirit of God is looking for like-minded and like-hearted individuals who will be the Daniels, the Esthers, the Josephs, and the Deborahs for their day. Like the biblical heroes before them, these modern-day trailblazers will study to show themselves approved as workmen for God, rightly dividing the word of truth (revelation) that is given to them (see 2 Tim. 2:15, KJV). And, like their Old Testament counterparts, they will learn to speak the language of that revelation in a manner that is relevant to their contemporaries.

What Language Do You Speak?

Before you can interpret your dreams properly or intercede effectively from the posture of revelation, you must understand the language of that revelation. In his book on dreams, Mark Rutland issues this caution:

> Believers must, of course, be cautious when seeking to understand dreams and even more prudent when acting on them. There is no substitute for wisdom and discernment in dream interpretation, and prayer is crucial to developing both. Believers should commit their subconscious minds to the Lord as well as their waking thoughts, then seek from God, in earnest prayer, understanding for the visions of the night.[126]

What language do you speak? Have you learned your spiritual alphabet? Your spiritual alphabet will be unique to you. God will speak revelation to you according to the language you speak. Doctors, nurses, and other medical and health professionals have a language all their own, a technical vocabulary that untrained laypeople cannot understand. Music has a written language that is incomprehensible to anyone who has never been taught to read the symbols. Pastors have their own language, too. This can cause problems when their language does not match that of their congregations!

What language do you speak? Whatever your language is, the Holy Spirit will speak to you in that language. Of course, I am not talking so much about languages like English, French, German, Russian, or Spanish, as I am the "language" with which we interpret life. Because each of us has different life experiences, the language by which we receive and impart revelation will be distinct to each of us. We each have a personal walk and, in a sense, a personal talk. Our spiritual alphabet, though similar, is unique to each individual.

Regardless of how our individual spiritual alphabets differ, our basic approach to interpretation should be the same. Proper interpretation can occur on many different levels. Here are three simple steps for interpreting your dream revelation:

1. Study the interpretation of words and symbols by research-ing their meanings as recorded in Scripture and other histor-ical literature. Find out how biblical characters and other figures from the past interpreted these words and symbols in a dream context. This is an excellent (and probably the easi-est) way to begin.

2. Develop the habit of journaling. Effective interpretation is a skill that is learned over time and with experience. Your spiri-tual alphabet is unique to you. Journaling will help you cap-ture your distinct pictures, grant understanding over time, and give wisdom for your journey.

3. Welcome the anointing, gifting, and presence of the Holy Spirit. He will guide you into truth, keeping things safe yet adventurous and pure yet unreligious.

In your eagerness to reach step three, don't bypass steps one and two. Always begin with the Scriptures. Let the Bible be its own best commentary. God will never contradict His Word. Let His written Word give you insight into the meaning of His visionary revelation. Study it thoroughly. Pray over it. Lay a solid foundation of the Word in your life to give the Holy Spirit something to breathe upon.

Interpreting dreams is like putting together a giant jigsaw puzzle with thousands of tiny pieces that must be fitted together in exactly the right order. As I mentioned in a previous chapter, the quickest way to complete a jigsaw puzzle is to start with the border—the framework—and the same is true with dream interpretation. Once you have the framework in place it becomes easier to see where the rest of the pieces go. Before long, the big picture begins to take shape. At least, that's the way it usually works for me. I ask the Holy Spirit to give me a thought or a word. He sheds His light on one thing, which leads me to another, and another, and then everything just starts to click.

Interpretations Belong to God

The cardinal rule to keep in mind when properly interpreting dreams and visions is that "interpretations belong to God." He who gives you the spirit of revelation is also the one who gives you the capacity to interpret that revelation. Here are some biblical examples:

From the life of Joseph: "*Then they said to him, 'We have had a dream and there is no one to interpret it.' Then Joseph said to them, 'Do not interpretations belong to God? Tell it to me, please.'*"[127] Imagine being in the place where you are so sure that interpretations belong to God and so absolutely confident in His anointing that, like Joseph, you could say to someone, "Tell it [your dream] to me," and know that God would give you the interpretation!

From the life of Daniel: "*As for these four youths, God gave them knowledge and intelligence in every branch of literature and wisdom; Daniel even understood all kinds of visions and dreams. ...As for every matter of wisdom and understanding about which the king consulted them, he found them ten times better than all the magicians and conjurers who were in all his realm.*"[128] Daniel was even given the ability to interpret the handwriting on the wall that King Belshazzar saw, which foretold the king's death under God's judgment.[129]

Although it may not come out in Aramaic or Hebrew or Greek or English or Spanish, God writes in signs to His people and He wants to give us the capacity to interpret the signs of the times. We need to pray for the Lord to release in our own day godly people of wisdom who can interpret the handwriting on the wall for our generation.

From the life of Issachar: "*Of the sons of Issachar, men who understood the times, with knowledge of what Israel should do, their chiefs were two hundred; and all their kinsmen were at their command.*"[130] Two hundred chiefs "*who understood the times*" held an entire tribe under their command. How? People will follow a person who has revelation. People will be drawn to anyone who walks with integrity in the spirit of wisdom and revelation.

The more you learn how to listen and recognize the voice of the Spirit of God, the more He will enable you to operate on multiple levels of insight. God is the master multitasker and He can enable you to be a multitasker as well. You can listen on more than one level. You can listen to the heart of a person, you can listen to the realm of the soul, and you can listen to the Holy Spirit. It requires a fair measure of grace and the ability to block out the noise of friction, static, and distractions, but all things are possible.

What God did before, He wants to do again! Right here, right now!

Revelation Is Full of Symbolism

Dreams are often the language of emotions and therefore contain much symbolism. We must learn to take our interpretations first from Scripture and then from our own lives. Throughout Scripture God is consistent with His symbolic language. The symbolism He uses in Genesis will be similar to that found in Revelation. In fact, one of the fundamental principles of biblical interpretation is the "law of first use." This simply means that how a word or image or symbol or type is used in its first appearance in Scripture is a key to how it should be interpreted throughout the Bible. This consistency in symbolic language runs true in our own lives as well.

Let me explain a little further. In the Bible, the number six often is used as a symbol for mankind. How do we know this? Refer back to the first chapter of Genesis. What happened on the sixth day of creation? Man was created. Day six is the day of man. Now let's go to the other end of the Bible, to the Book of Revelation. There we find the reference to the number 666, which is plainly identified as *"the number of a man."*[131] In the Greek there is no definite article preceding the word for "man" in this verse, so it could also be translated simply as "the number of man." The number 666 represents a false trinity, the exaltation of man; humanism being worshiped as a god. In both Genesis and Revelation, therefore, the number six is associated with mankind.

Here is another similar example. What happened on the seventh day of creation? God rested because He had finished His creative work. Therefore, the number seven is the number of rest or completion. According to the four Gospels combined, how many statements did Jesus make from the cross? Seven. The last of these was, *"It is finished!"*[132] Jesus had finished His work; He had completed His mission. Now He could rest. Throughout the Bible the number seven is symbolically associated with rest and completion.

A similar principle applies when God speaks revelation to you. When He first introduces a word or a symbol or an image to you in a dream, you may not understand it in the beginning. But you will get it eventually, and that word, symbol, or image will become part of a pattern. Once it is introduced into your spiritual alphabet, it will become consistent in its meaning for you. For example, let's say that you have a dream in which an apple appears and you discern through the Holy Spirit that it symbolizes Israel because Zechariah 2:8 refers to Israel as the "apple" of God's eye. Once the image of the apple has entered your spiritual alphabet as a symbol for Israel, you can be confident that whenever that image appears in a future dream, the dream has something to do with the nation of Israel. God is consistent with His revelatory symbolism.

Three Realms for Interpretation of Symbols

When seeking interpretation of symbolic dream language, the first place you should look *always* is in Scripture. The Bible is full of parables and allegories from which to draw types, shadows, and symbols. Here are some examples: the mustard seed as a metaphor for faith;[133] incense representing the prayers of the saints;[134] seed as a symbol for the Word of God[135]; and candlesticks symbolizing the church.[136] If your dream has the same symbolic image as one found in the Bible, chances are it has the same meaning.

After Scripture, a second place to look for interpretation of dream symbols is in colloquial expressions that fill our memory bank. The Holy Spirit turns these into pictorial language. God takes these "sayings" and idioms and uses them to speak spiritual truth. One example of this is found in Judges 7:9-15 where a barley cake appears to Gideon in a dream. Since Gideon had spent much of his life as a thresher of wheat and barley, the barley cake was a symbol from his colloquial spiritual alphabet and had distinct meaning to him.

In the same way, God will speak to you with colloquial expressions that are familiar to you but might not be to someone else. If you are from the northern or northeastern part of the country, your colloquialisms will be different than those of someone from the Deep South, and God will speak to each of you accordingly.

The third realm for interpreting dream symbols comes from our own personal revelatory alphabet. This is similar to the second realm in that the objects or symbols do not mean the same thing to you as they would to someone else. Even in the Bible the same symbol or image sometimes means something different depending on how it is used or who receives it. These exceptions, however, do *not* violate the law of first use.

God often works more than one way at a time. And sometimes the symbol or image involved has more than one facet or aspect, which allows for some variations in meaning. Context determines interpretation.

The Bible uses the image of a lamb in several different ways. In Isaiah, the Messiah is presented as a *Lamb* led to the slaughter. John's Gospel presents Jesus as the Good Shepherd and His disciples as *little lambs*. The Book of Revelation reveals Jesus Christ the *Lamb* as a Conqueror. Spiritually speaking, all three of these images are true to a lamb's nature: it is led to the slaughter, it follows its shepherd, and it conquers in the end by walking in humility because the meek will inherit the earth.

Actual Versus Visual

Insights, revelations, warnings, and prophecies from the Lord may come in supernatural *visual* dreams or in *actual* dreams.[137] Visual dreams are visual revelations that do not involve as much active participation on the part of the dreamer as with an actual visitation from the Lord. The dreamer simply observes and receives the message. These visual dreams may contain more symbols, mysteries, and obscurities than do other types of revelation.

Actual dreams are those in which God's tangible presence is evident in some way. To see the Lord in a dream is *visual,* but for the Lord to *manifest* Himself to you in a dream is *actual.* If you dream something angelic and sense that same presence when you wake up, it was more than just a *visual symbolic* dream. The angels were *actually* there. Quite often this will reveal itself in the form of a riveting awareness all over your body of a divine presence in the room. But if there was *no* such manifested presence when you awakened, then the dream was simply *visual,* although it may still contain a message from God.

A manifestation of blessing, healing, deliverance, or endowment of power requires an *actual* visitation from the Lord in some form. Such manifestations involve an impartation of God's anointing, which will manifest in the natural realm. Therefore, an *actual impartation* occurs and the person actively participates although his or her body is asleep.

I have vivid memories of some dream encounters that I call "the Bread of His Presence" dreams. In one of them I was carrying loaves of bread and was searching for the little mint-green blanket that belonged to our daughter Rachel. Rachel loved that blanket and for quite a few years carried it with her just about everywhere she went. In my dream, I found Rachel's blanket and wrapped the loaves of bread in it. I held them closely to my chest and noticed that the bottom of each loaf was a little satin napkin that looked like a diaper.

This was an *actual* dream because there was an *actual* presence in the room. I was asleep, but the Holy Spirit was very active. Even asleep I was talking out loud and prophesying. This was more than just a message I passively received. I declared, "Just as we parents learn to love, nurture, care for, and cherish our newborn child, so should we as believers care for, love, and cherish the bread of God's presence, then revival will come."

When I woke up, my arms were outstretched over my chest as though I was clutching those loaves of bread tightly to my chest as if they were my very own babies, wrapped in my daughter's blanket. Even as I woke I heard myself prophesying, "When we as parents will care for, love, and nourish the bread of His presence, like a parent does his newborn child, then we will have revival." In fact, I was the one who was being revived. I loved God's presence just as I had our newborn child. Though I did not see any angels in the room upon waking, the manifested presence of God was so strong you could almost cut it with a knife! Yes, let's love the bread of His presence!

Some Basics of Dream Interpretation

Now it is time to get down to some "nuts and bolts" basics of dream interpretation. The first principle to keep in mind is to *reduce the dream to its simplest form*. With too much detail you could miss the interpretation. That is like not seeing the forest for the trees. Keep it simple. Otherwise, you risk obscuring the meaning. Take the dream to its simplest form and build on that.

Next, remember that *context determines interpretation*. The meaning is not always the same every time. For example, a seed can mean faith, the Word, the kingdom of God, a future harvest, etc. There are no steadfast formulas. The things of the Spirit are "spiritually discerned," not naturally discerned.[138]

Third, *determine whether a series of repetitious dreams is involved*. Did you have two, three, or four dreams, or are they all different aspects of the same issue? More than one dream in the same night is often just a different look or version of the same message. Joseph in the Book of Genesis had two dreams, each with different symbols, but both dreams had the same meaning. Whether it was sheaves of wheat in the field or the sun, moon, and stars in the heavens, both dreams meant that the members of Joseph's family would one day bow down to him. Joseph's dreams related to his destiny.

If you don't understand that repetitive dreams typically relate to the same subject matter, you will end up looking at them as entirely isolated dreams that have no connection to each other. In doing so you risk misinterpreting all of them. If you experience repetitive dreams, look for a common thread of meaning.

Analyze your dream by asking a series of basic questions. First, *are you observing?* Where are you in the dream? If you are in the observation mode, then the dream probably is not primarily about you. It is about someone or somewhere else. God does nothing without a witness observing issues. If you are an observer in your dream, then you are that witness. This might even mean that you are going to be a watchman or an intercessor in the situation.

Second, *are you participating?* Are you actively participating in the dream but still not the main figure? Then the dream still is not primarily about you, even though its meaning may touch you more directly than when you are merely an observer.

Third, *are you the focus?* Is everyone watching you? If you are the focus of the dream, then one of the first things you need to do is try to identify where you are. That will help you frame out the dream so all the pieces can be put into place.

Fourth, *what are the objects, thoughts, and emotions in the dream?* Are there words in the dream? What impressions and thoughts are you left with when you remember or are awakened by the dream? What is the intensity of the dream—the main emotion? You will know intuitively what the most important issues are.

Interpreting Colors in Dreams

Understanding the significance and use of colors is one of the key principles to proper interpretation. Colors can have both a good and positive meaning as well as an opposite bad or negative meaning. Remember, context is the key! Dreams are full of these understandings; they are often

143

descriptive parables of light. Let's go to *The Seer* book once again for some illustrations. Here are some representative examples:

1. *Amber*—the glory of God (Ezek. 1:4; 8:2, KJV).

2. *Black*—sin, death, and famine (Lam. 4:8; Rev. 6:5; Jer. 8:21).

3. *Blue*—Heaven, Holy Spirit (Num. 15:38).

4. *Crimson/Scarlet*—blood atonement, sacrifice (Isa. 1:18; Lev. 14:52; Josh. 2:18,21).

5. *Purple*—kingship, royalty (John 19:2; Judg. 8:26).

6. *Red*—bloodshed, war (Rev. 6:4; 12:3; 2 Kings 3:22).

7. *White*—purity, light, righteousness (Rev. 6:2; 7:9).

Interpreting Numbers in Dreams

Like colors, numbers are highly significant both in the Bible as well as in dreams. So it is important to learn a few basic principles for interpreting numbers. If you internalize and follow the principles, they will help preserve you from interpretation error or extremes.

1. The simple numbers of 1-13 often have specific spiritual significance.

2. Multiples of these numbers, or doubling or tripling, carries basically the same meaning, only they intensify the truth.

3. The first use of the number in Scripture generally conveys its spiritual meaning (the law of first use).

4. Consistency of interpretation. God is consistent, and what a number means in Genesis is the same thing that it means through all Scripture to Revelation.

5. The spiritual significance is not always stated, but may be veiled, or hidden, or seen by comparison with other Scriptures.

6. Generally, there are good and evil, true and counterfeit, godly and satanic aspects in numbers.

Getting a little more specific, let's look at the numbers 1-13 and their possible symbolic meanings:

1. One: God, beginning, source (Gen. 1:1).

2. Two: witness, testimony (John 8:17; Matt. 18:16; Deut. 17:6).

3. Three: Godhead, divine completeness (Ezek. 14:14-18; Dan. 3:23-24).

4. Four: earth, creation, winds, seasons (Gen. 2:10; 1 Cor. 15:39).

5. Five: Cross, grace, atonement (Gen. 1:20-23; Lev. 1:5; Eph. 4:11).

6. Six: man, beast, satan (Gen. 1:26-31; 1 Sam. 17:4-7; Num. 35:15).

7. Seven: perfection, completeness (Heb. 6:1-2; Judg. 14; Josh. 6).

8. Eight: new beginning (Gen. 17; 1 Pet. 3:20; 2 Pet. 3:8).

9. Nine: finality, fullness (Matt. 27:45; Gen. 7:1-2; Gal. 5:22-23; 1 Cor. 12:1-12).

10. Ten: law, government (Exod. 34:28).

11. Eleven: this organization, lawlessness, Antichrist (Dan. 7:24; Gen. 32:22).

12. Twelve: defying government, apostolic fullness (Exod. 28:21; Matt. 10:2-5; Lev. 24:5-6).

13. Thirteen: rebellion, backsliding, apostasy (Gen. 14:4; 1 Kings 11:6).

Two Other Factors to Consider

Dream interpretation is also affected by culture. There are cultural and social interpretations that we must bring into our understanding as well: West versus East; North versus South; North American versus South American; European versus African; Middle Eastern versus Asian; Chinese versus Russian, etc. The degree to which you have to consider these cultural factors will depend on your sphere of influence. The larger your sphere, the more significance these cultural elements will have for you.

Another critical key to dream interpretation that is sometimes overlooked is the discipline of meditating on the Word of God:

When I remember You on my bed, I meditate on You in the night watches. [139]

I will meditate on all Your work and muse on Your deeds. [140]

I will meditate on Your precepts and regard Your ways. [141]

I remember the days of old; I meditate on all Your doings; I muse on the work of Your hands. [142]

Take the time to gain understanding of the principles and metaphors of Scripture. Like the psalmist, meditate on them day and night. They can have many layers of meaning.

Keeping Interpretation Simple

Walking in dream language and tapping into the mind and heart of God can be an exciting and exhilarating journey. But understanding and interpreting the revelation He gives in dreams can often be a complex and even confusing process. Therefore, let me summarize what we have discussed in a handful of concise statements that will make everything easier to remember.

1. Most of all, dreams should be interpreted on a personal basis first (John 10:3).

2. Most dreams should not be taken literally. They need interpretation (Dan. 1:17; Gen. 40:8).

3. God will use familiar terms that you know (Matt. 4:19).

4. Ponder on the dream or revelation and ask the Holy Spirit for insight (Dan. 7:8; 8:15-16; Luke 2:19; 1 Cor. 2:10-12).

5. Ask the Holy Spirit what the central thought, word, or issue is in the revelation. Reduce the dream to its simplest form. What is the main thought?

6. Search it out in the Word. Dreams from the Lord will never go against His written Word (Prov. 25:2).

7. What did you sense and feel from the dream? Was it a good or evil presence? What was the primary emotion?

8. Relate the dream to your circumstances and spheres of influence.

9. Consecutive dreams often have similar meanings (Gen. 41:1-7, 25-31). God will speak the same message more than once in more than one way.

10. What are the colors? Is everything black and white with one main object in color?

11. Interpretations can be on three levels: personal, church, or national and international.

12. More than one interpretation can come forth in one dream. Just as with Scripture, there is the historical context as well as the personal, present implication. So it is with dreams. It might be a general word for the church with specific applications for yourself (or others).

13. Some dreams may only be understood in the future. They unfold over time. Details will make sense down the road.

14. Write down in a journal the summary; date it; write down where you were, the time (if you woke up from it), the main emotions, and a possible interpretation.

15. The key to proper interpretation is to ask questions, questions, questions!

Finally, remember that dreams are significant to all! There couldn't be a society of people who didn't dream. They'd be dead in two weeks.[143] To receive a dream is the human obligation that begins to move a divine purpose from the mind of God to become reality in human history.[144]

Dreams are where space and time are pushed away, where God allows our inner selves to see beyond and behind the conscious plane and where possibilities and hopes, as well as all our hidden monsters, come out, come out wherever they are.

Dreaming permits each and every one of us to be quietly and safely insane every night of our lives.[145]

But life is more than dreams. As author Mark Rutland says:

If we idolize the primary mental image and cling to it too tenaciously, we may well despise the realization of the dream when it finally arrives. An overly cherished fantasy has the capacity to steal our joy and even blind us to the dreams for which we have longed.[146]

In closing, let us consider the cautionary wisdom of "The Preacher" in Ecclesiastes: *"For in many dreams and in many words there is emptiness. Rather, fear God."*[147]

Father, we know that dreams and their interpretations belong to You. With honor coupled with a deep hunger, we ask You to give us Your wisdom applications, in Jesus' great name, Amen.

Reflection Questions

1. Proper interpretation can occur on many different levels. What are the three basic methods for interpreting your dream revelation?

2. What does the idea that "context determines interpretation" mean to you? How does this work?

3. In keeping interpretation simple, what are some of the 15 ways listed?

Referral Reading

Ira Milligan, *Understanding the Dreams You Dream* (Shippensburg, PA: Destiny Image, 1997).

Herman Riffel, *Dream Interpretation* (Shippensburg, PA: Destiny Image, 1993).

Kevin Connor, *Interpreting Symbols and Types* (Portland, OR: Bible Temple Publications, 1989).

PART THREE

WALKING IN WISDOM

In this final section I will focus on journaling, the silence of God, and learning to handle dreams with wisdom.

Journaling is a tried and tested spiritual tool that will help you retain revelation and grow in your capacity to discern the voice of the Holy Spirit. Basically, journaling is simply a tool for keeping notes for future reference. Journaling is a major key to remembering. I know that all of you have awakened in the morning and then later in the day tried to remember what you have dreamed and could not. Dreams can escape us, and the key to capturing dreams is in the spiritual privilege called journaling.

In the middle of this last section I dedicate a whole chapter to the silence of God. This is a precious chapter to me, close to my very heart.

In the midst of talking about revelation, dreams, and visions, and the many ways that God talks to us, we must sit down, take a breath, and remember one critical thing about the Christian walk. There are those times when there are no visions, no dreams, and no seeming answers to prayers—only silence. The prophet Isaiah once declared, "*Truly, You are a God who hides Himself, O God of Israel, Savior!*" (Isa. 45:15). The Jewish theologians call this the Mask of Yahweh. Both David and Job cried out to God in bewilderment at His silence, "Why dost thou hide Thy face?"

What do you do in those moments when you are walking through a dry place? When God seems silent, recognize this as His invitation to you to come into greater union with Christ. God's silence is His way of calling you to press in. When your dreams seem to fade away, press in—because the God of dreams has not faded away. He is always there waiting to embrace you and to expand your heart's capacity to receive more of His Word, His will, and His ways. When God seems silent, press in!

In the closing chapter, I will remind you that revelation is hot stuff! Like a pot of boiling water on a stove, it can burn you if you mishandle it. Always put on your "mittens" of wisdom before trying to carry your cargo of revelation to its place of usefulness and purpose. Otherwise, it might spill on you! So, in this chapter I will offer you the "gloves" of wisdom. These are words of wisdom that have been formed through many years of experience. I have learned wisdom in many different ways, but like you, some of my lessons have been learned the hard way. When dealing with dreams, visions, and revelation, we will each surely need to know the wisdom ways of God.

Keep reading—wisdom for your journey is right around the corner!

CHAPTER NINE

STOPS ALONG THE WAY
(BY MICHAL ANN GOLL)

Exploring this "new world" of dreams requires a few tools to make your way through the many, and I do mean many, trails and avenues. Tom Sawyer had a string that he used, when he was trying to find his way through that cave, that if he got lost, he could at least make it back to the point of familiarity. Jim and I have explored this ground extensively, and in the process, have found some real nuggets of wisdom and insight.

Therefore, in preparation for the next chapter, which will examine journaling in detail, I would like in this chapter to share with you some more stops along my dream journey. None of this would have been possible had I not developed the habit of journaling my dreams and recording the insights and understanding that have come to me over time.

I always enjoy reading back through my journals. The images, experiences, and insights written in them are like treasures and precious jewels to me. Some of these dreams were incredibly powerful, including some *actual* dreams that were delivered by angelic hosts who were actually present in my bedroom. Even today, when I read some of my journal entries, my body starts to tremble and my lips tingle as if the angels have come and touched them again and once more imparted a message from God.

Let me begin by sharing one of those *actual* dreams with you—a dream personally delivered by angels.

Kansas City Activation

This dream occurred years ago while we were still living in Kansas City. We had been through an incredible amount of spiritual warfare. It was as if our house was under the downspout of a huge hollow tube that had its source in the kingdom of darkness and all that vile sewage was being dumped right on top of us. It was a very dark and very difficult period in our lives.

During this time Jim got quite sick and hallucinated for about ten days. We were in the midst of trying to show and sell our house ourselves. All four of our children were still small. One day I started feeling ill as well. I had a fever and soon discovered that I was also experiencing occasional blackouts—there were periods of time that I could not account for. At times my fever ran as high as 104 or 105 degrees.

Even my doctor did not know what was going on at first. Eventually, I was hospitalized with a very unusual kind of double pneumonia that had settled in the upper part of my lungs, instead of the lower, which is one reason they had trouble finding it. The pneumonia was so severe that I spent two weeks in the hospital. We had to ship our children out for our family to take care of. This was especially hard because Rachel was just a baby. I was away from my children for about six weeks! That was one of the most painful parts of this time.

Once I came home from the hospital I was so weak that I could barely lift a coffee mug. I would get up at ten o'clock in the morning and by two in the afternoon was so exhausted I was ready to go back to bed. This was only a few days before a major conference that we were planning to attend.

One morning I had a dream where an oppressor was trying to get everyone to turn away from Jesus. I was one of the leaders of this Jesus group. My life was being threatened. If I refused to renounce Jesus, I could be killed. I turned and looked at the people in my group, knowing that my decision would affect how they responded.

We all stood up and started singing a song to Jesus. At that point an enemy soldier came over and struck me on the top of the head with the butt of his rifle. When this happened in the dream, there was an actual experience outside of the dream. It was like the dream opened the doorway for the next step, as the dream ended and I entered into the following experience. Instantly, my head "split open" figuratively from shafts of revelation light. I sat up in bed, fully aware that an angel was present in my room. It was four in the morning, yet I was totally energized with what I can only describe as circles and circles of revelation light. I was so activated that I could not stay in bed. I jumped up, not even knowing what to do with myself.

I could not sit down and I could not lie down. I was totally wired from the download of this dream, which involved a word that I was supposed to give to Daniel Brymer, the leader of the worship team of the church that was hosting the upcoming conference. I had this feeling of *knowing* that the members of the worship team were to be like warplanes that God was going to send to drop bombs on the enemy's territory. I felt an overwhelming sense of urgency to call, but it was too early in the morning; yet neither could I just sit and wait.

I was on pins and needles like that all day long. At an appropriate hour I phoned Daniel and told him about my dream. I said, "You are like warplanes. Your whole team is going to go up into the heavens and drop bombs of praise." He received all this with great excitement and was totally energized. The Lord used this experience to launch that worship team into such a higher plane of purpose and anointing—it was awesome! All the praise and worship music at that conference was recorded, and the resulting tapes are some of the most anointed warfare praise and worship that I have ever heard. By the way, I continued to be energized and, despite my recent illness, was able to attend that first night's meeting. I was buzzing! Yea, God!

Seeds of Burden Bearing

In addition to spiritual warfare dreams, I have had many major destiny dreams. These dreams are like God impregnating you with holy seeds so that you give birth to things in the Spirit. God loves to use language that we know and understand, and what better analogy than looking at the incubation period of gestation of our own children. When the announcement of that cherished and anticipated birth is first given, our natural question is, "What will this baby look like? Will he/she look like the mother or the father?"

This is a natural question, but there is a similar question as to burdens/births we help to carry through dreams and intercession. We never know what those holy seeds will grow up to look like. We never know in advance where they will take us. Dreams of destiny enlarge our heart and our perspective. Our identity expands beyond ourselves until we identify with the entire world. I like to call these "seeds of burden bearing." The following are some of these impacting dreams. I will not try to bring detailed interpretation to these dreams here, as my main purpose is just to let the dreams unfold and let the Spirit of God stir you as He desires.

The World's Heartbeat

This dream came to me on March 31, 1989. In my dream, nuclear war had taken place, and even though it was a "limited" war, damage and exposure to radiation were extensive. Members of my family had been exposed to radiation, and some had actually died. Like everyone else, I too had been exposed and was expected to become terminally ill. Yet somehow I escaped harm.

The scene changed, and I became aware that the earth was in imminent danger of total destruction unless we interceded in prayer long enough and hard enough. The problem was in getting others to respond. I remember looking out a window at night when suddenly a shuddering vibration swept through the house. I thought, *This is it!* It was not a bomb but some sort of super aircraft powerful enough and fast enough to circle the globe from north to south and wrap it with an invisible cord so strong that as it tightened it would literally cut the world in two, plunging it into everlasting destruction.

I felt the earth collapsing from underneath my feet. As I fell, I saw the earth in its normal position and heard a steady heartbeat. A moment later, the earth split and the heartbeat stopped. I saw a woman ready to give birth floating on her back in space. She was lamenting uncontrollably. Her abdomen had been opened somehow, as if by an explosion, and she held in her hands the small bloody earth. It was as though she had been unable to carry it to full term and now it was dead.

Once again the scene changed. We were in a large city at nighttime and the threat of missile attack was imminent. Suddenly, there was a flash. We could see the missile chasing us, and it was as though somehow we were riding on a missile of our own, trying to get away. Somehow, we escaped detection and the missile lost its target. We celebrated, laughed, and danced in the relief that it was all over.

This is probably a dream of End-Time magnitude. It is surely a dream calling His people to spiritual warfare!

The War in Iraq—February 1991

During Operation Desert Storm, I had a dream where I saw part of a map of Iraq, with two dotted lines coming down from the top to form a "V" toward Baghdad. I thought possibly that they represented two roads that led to Baghdad, but Jim thought they symbolized the Tigris and the Euphrates rivers and the point where they converge.

I observed a Jeep-like vehicle carrying four people racing down the road trying to reach the airport at the convergence point in order to escape Iraq. The phrase came to me that they had to go through Iran to get there. I believe it was a play on words, "I ran." Before they could make good their escape, however, a military vehicle appeared behind them with a light flashing on the top.

Suddenly, I was no longer just an observer but was in the Jeep with them. Immediately I began crying out to the Lord to destroy the enemy so that no harm would come to us. Before long, the enemy vehicle ran off the road, turned over, and was destroyed.

Finally, the Jeep reached the end of the road, but the passengers found no airport. I was in observer mode once again. The passengers decided that a plane was coming at a certain time to airlift them out. Little did they know that only a few hundred feet away hundreds of Iraqi troops were huddled in trenches. The Iraqis captured them, brought them into a room, and told them that the only way the four of them would be set free was if one of them volunteered to allow the Iraqis to place some sort of chemical acid on his or her hand.

One of the women agreed. The Iraqi leader advised her to look at the other people in the room before she made her final decision. As I watched the scene I noticed several people whose faces were horribly altered. Their skin was ashen gray and hung so loosely on their faces that all you could see were their expressionless eyes and long thin mouths.

At this sight the female volunteer changed her mind. But the soldiers grabbed her, held her down by force, and told her they were going to put acid on her face. She was terrified, but it turned out to be only water.

157

This was mental torture, all part of the spirit of terror that was being released.

The soldiers did actually put some acid on the inner calf of one man's right leg. His skin grew white and swollen, and they promised him release, as he had fulfilled the requirement for someone to volunteer.

Finally, the plane arrived, but they had to walk a long distance to get to it, which was extremely difficult for the man with the acid-burned leg to do. They made him walk up a long flight of stairs and down a long walk to the plane. When he was almost there they closed the door in his face. He stood at the door, pounding it with his fist and demanding that they let him in, which they finally did.

The plane finally took off, yet there was no assurance that they were safe because the Iraqis had no air cover. The allied forces did not know who was on the plane and would surely try to bring it down. I never saw the plane crash; it simply disappeared over the horizon.

For me, that dream was a major call to prayer. My vision of that plane kept me continually before the Lord on behalf of our soldiers and everyone caught up in that conflict. Jim, under the Lord's direction, had set aside his normal schedule for the entire period of the Gulf War. For that entire month our lives were on pause and we were watchers on the wall for the cradle of civilization.

Three Jewish Men

In this dream, three tall, black-bearded Jewish men stood in front of me with their arms folded, saying, "Who do you think you are that God would use you to bring good news to the Jewish people? You are nothing, a nobody." I looked at them and replied, "You're absolutely right. I am a nobody. It is only by the grace of God and by His anointing that anybody does anything."

I then began praying to the Lord, and a spirit of supplication came over me. "Oh Lord," I cried out, "please release Your anointing so that the good news can be released. Only You can do this, Lord. Please shine down Your revelation light."

Immediately a light from Heaven shone down on me like a spotlight, plainly visible for everyone to see. The three Jewish men took a step back, clapped their hands to their mouths, and said, "Oh, we see!" It was like they suddenly saw the favor of the Lord on me and changed their position.

Indeed, this was a dream of destiny and calling. God does want to use us to bring good news to the Jewish people, but for me this dream was all about my taking the low road and saying, "You're right. I am nobody; I am nothing." The Lord has used this approach many times to teach me how to do spiritual warfare. You don't go head-to-head with the enemy. You recognize that you are nobody and then you simply exalt Jesus.

Shackles Transformed

In another dream I saw shackles on Jews' ankles coming off and being transformed into beautifully and intricately carved ivory bracelets. Basically, that was it. There is no standard or formula for length of revelatory dreams. Some are quite lengthy while others are nothing more than "snapshots." God wants to change all our shackles into tokens of His bridal adornment. He can turn anything around!

The Well-Blended Woman

This is a dream first related to me years ago by Penny Kaeding, a personal friend who also has a ministry that is associated with ours. This was a dream that the Lord gave to Penny about me. Penny describes her dream experience as it is told from my viewpoint:

> I saw oil refineries burning all over the world. I was involved in visiting these different places, handing out blankets and food. Before long I became so overwhelmed with the crushing need of the people that I did not know what to do. In the end I was thrown into this big blender, and it was turned on. I guess it evened out all my "lumps" or something, because I came out smooth. The phrase that I heard in my dream was that I was a "well-blended woman" who was no longer overwhelmed but used by God to release His goodness, blessings, and mercy. This was years before I ever had even a thought about a ministry of compassion, years before I had any idea that I would be involved in some way in working with relief.

At that time Penny and I were getting ready to go to Israel. We took rollerblades with us as a prophetic act so that we could get around to all those different refineries, in a spiritual way, and make tracks—because Israel was supposed to be the beginning point where all this was going to be launched. We ended up launching something and didn't even know what it was we launched. But it was the ministry of the "well-blended woman," and it was definitely a God thing.

Although this dream is a calling dream, it is a teaching or instructional dream as well. We are all called to be well-blended believers bringing many ingredients together for His name's sake.

Baby Jesus

In this dream, Jim and I seemed to be in Israel. All around us were narrow dusty roads and passageways, stone houses built together and connected in a line, separated only by stone walls. Jim seemed heartsick; he wanted to talk to people about Jesus but was so moved by what he saw that he could not participate in any conversations.

The scene shifted and it was as though we had gone back in time. An army of foot and horse soldiers was ready to march into the city. A sense of panic filled the air. People were scurrying everywhere, trying to get out of the city before it was captured. Most had already fled, but Jim and I were staying. We were dressed in old garments, long robes like in Bible times. It seemed we had no place to go; besides, we felt that we were supposed to stay. We were just sitting there in our little stone house, waiting for the enemy to enter the city.

I walked over to the window. As I looked out, a horse-drawn cart in the street below was just passing in front of our house. The people in the cart appeared to be fleeing and needed refuge. I called to them from the window: "Master, wait, wait." The cart was moving so fast that by the time I spoke it had already traveled past our place. I thought the occupants had not heard me. But then I heard the hoofbeats slowing down. I saw the cart stop, turn around, and come back to our house. A man and a woman got off the cart and came into our house and sat down. The woman was holding a small bundle. As she sat down she opened the bundle, and I saw that it was the baby Jesus.

Great things begin in small packages. You might be impatient for your ministry to take off, but wait. Yes, wait. What He says He will do— He will birth it in His good timing!

"My Body Is a Dismembered Body"

This dream occurred on October 28, 1989. I was in a small country church, much like Wallace Chapel, the little Methodist church where I grew up. The service was in progress, and I saw myself lying on a pew with a pillow and blanket, sick from pregnancy. As the service continued, a huge windstorm gradually began to overtake us. Eventually, we were completely surrounded and enveloped by this storm. Even as the wind grew, I sensed a tremendous spirit of prophecy coming upon me and filling me. I had no fear of what was going on around me because the Word of the Lord was coming forth from me and I could see His purpose in this storm.

By this time in the dream I was no longer sick and had no fear of death or harm of any kind at any time. The church building rattled and shook and actually began to tumble end over end until the walls were falling, collapsing around us. People were afraid and seemed to rally around me. Barriers between people were broken; we knew we needed each other.

A man named Bill Greenman was there. Bill is a personal friend who represents to me the spirit of faith. We hugged each other tightly for a long time and drew strength from each other, bonding together tremendously in the Spirit.

By the time the storm finally stopped, the entire front wall of the church was gone. Symbolically, this is what the Lord is doing in the church today. He is knocking the front of the church off, getting us out of the four walls. People were confused and wanting to know what to do. Everything seemed to be in total chaos. And yet the peace of the Lord and the Word of the Lord was resting heavily upon me. I told everyone not to worry and that we would make it out of this situation. Even as I spoke, I saw through the ruins of the church building to the outside world, which was a beautiful, scenic countryside, green with spring grass. A tree-lined creek meandered through a pasture, while the sounds of birds singing and frogs croaking filled the wonderful fresh air.

Before everyone had exited the church, however, I looked to the west and, in a very loud and commanding voice, declared the Word of the Lord to the Truman Sports Complex located in Kansas City, Missouri. I don't recall what I said, but I sensed judgment coming against it, and even a caution for Christians to not go there lest they be found there at the wrong time and judgment come on them as well.

The words proceeded out of my mouth and sped with great power and speed to their destination, splitting the heavens and leaving a trail of smoke in their path. All at once, I and the rest of the people who had been in the church seemed to be translated to Kansas City. We entered the apartment of some friends and began talking with them. However, I was unable to enter into any of the conversations because the Spirit was so heavy upon me. I sensed that something very traumatic was about to happen.

I looked out the window. That is when I felt the earthquake. I don't know if the building actually shook, but I felt it inside. Our little group rushed outside and watched as people began streaming out of the other buildings. They emerged like something was driving them out, the way roaches come out of the walls when the exterminator sprays the house. The people were fine when they came out, but almost before I saw them I spoke out very clearly and powerfully, "The arms are coming apart! The elbow is being disjointed from the lower arm! The wrist and hand are falling apart! The knees are disjointed, and the legs and ankles are becoming separated."

As I said this, it was actually happening to the people. They were literally falling apart before our eyes. In great distress and travail I cried out, "My body is a dismembered body!" The pain and anguish of the Lord was so severe that I was sobbing terribly and yet at the same time God granted me great healing power. I would point my finger at someone's dismembered ankle, and as I focused with my eyes it was as though laser surgery was performed from my eyes through my fingers, and healing immediately took place. This happened many times.

Then we walked down a narrow street with tall, close buildings on either side and came to a cul-de-sac. It was very rundown and neglected. I had a strong sense that it was in the inner city. As we neared the cul-de-sac, people began crying to us from within the buildings, "Is there still time for us? Will Jesus care for us too? Will He accept us?" These people were the down and the destitute, full of incurable diseases, AIDS, cancer, etc. There were drug users, addicts, people who were not in their right mind; it was like a modern-day lepers' colony. They had been confined, almost as though imprisoned, and had lost all hope. Immediately, in the power of the Spirit of the Lord, I proclaimed with great authority the Good News of the gospel. As I began preaching, thousands poured out of the buildings and surrounded us.

Jim was with me. He was in the center, holding his Bible in his hands in front of him. I knew he was praying silently. I continued to preach until suddenly all I heard was Carl Tuttle leading us in worship, singing "Lord, You Are Holy." The presence of the Lord was so strong that it seemed no one could say or sing anything else. Nothing else mattered.

When I woke up, my spirit was so stirred that I spent an hour or more crying and quietly praying to the Lord. I knew He had spoken to me and imparted something of great worth. I also recall that He warned me about people looking at God's gift or burden on a person and incorrectly perceiving that as being part of the person's personality or strength, rather than seeing that person as one of God's vessels who is simply carrying the Lord's cargo.

There is yet coming a time when the Lord will release another level of faith and supernatural power to His Body. The Church will be healed physically and spiritually as the dismembered Body of Christ comes together and receives His heart for the outcast, the poor, and the disenfranchised.

Two Brothers

On January 11, 1994, I dreamed that Jim and I were in Europe, probably Germany, exploring a quaint little town. All the homes were two stories tall but small, and with bedrooms so small that many of the children had to sleep on old wooden floors because of lack of space. In one home lived two brothers, one sensible and one who was a little crazy. As time progressed, however, the sensible brother, because of his rigidity, began to go crazy while his crazy brother, because of his freedom, became sane.

Moses and the Masons

This is probably one of the wildest, most unusual dreams I have ever had. It was like a re-enactment of Moses' leading the Israelites to the Promised Land. At first I thought Moses was white and the Israelites were black, but I later realized that the people were very stubborn and contentious. They did not want to go and would not follow Moses' lead.

When he had told them not to go in a certain direction, they had refused to listen and had gotten themselves mired in a sticky, oily, tar-like substance. They were totally covered with it, as if they had rolled around in it. Their hair was matted to their heads. They could not get it out; it would have to wear off. This was their appearance and condition throughout the whole dream.

Moses was having a terrible time trying to lead these people. They were looking for a particular kind of berry and had come to the top of a very large mountain ridge, where a sign read, "Entering Slovakia." At the time I seemed to have the understanding that they were entering Czechoslovakia. Now I'm not so sure, but I think this was before Czechoslovakia was divided into Slovakia and the Czech Republic.

As they stood at the top of this ridge, Moses saw a pinkish hue in the valley below. He tried to lead the people down there, knowing that they would find the fruit there. But the people didn't want to go with him, so they scattered and went in various directions. Moses went on by himself toward the fruit. When he got there he saw that these berries, which looked like raspberries, were lying about four inches thick all along the bottom and up the sides of the valley. He scooped them up in handfuls and put them in sacks.

Finally, the people wandered over to where Moses was and decided that they now wanted the berries. Now that Moses had gathered them, he wanted to carry them someplace. But the people tried to take them away from him and ended up fighting among themselves, ripping the bags, spilling the fruit, and making a mess of everything.

Then the scene changed to a class of young teenage boys and girls who were very contentious among themselves. This was like two different dreams that were coming in separate packages but with the same message. Two girls were doing a mock shoot-out in the classroom with play guns. They acted like it was pretend, but I saw that in their hearts they really wanted to kill each other.

At one point two teams were going to play basketball. One team was noticeably weaker and fewer in number than the other team. There were two teachers; one was good and the other was not. The good teacher decided to play on the weaker team to help even the odds. When the other teacher heard about this, he decided to join the stronger team. He wanted that team to have an unfair advantage.

There was another situation where a brother had removed a part of his sister's bicycle and hidden it in his desk. She needed to go home but couldn't unless she rode her bike. Her bicycle would not operate without the missing part. She knew where it was and asked her brother to give it to her, but he refused.

At the end of the dream all the students in the class were in a kitchen area working on various projects. Three-fourths of the students started singing a song that went something like this: "We are part of the Masons, all hail and all glory be to the rituals of the Masons. We glorify the Masons." The other fourth of the class, about four students total, turned and looked at each other in the eye. They came to a sudden realization of who they were. With the new confidence that rose up in them, they lifted up one song in unison: "All praise be to Jesus, all glory be to Jesus, we believe in Jesus." It was as if they didn't know or realize who they were until they heard the other group singing about the Masons.

May the deception be exposed. May a deliverer like unto Moses appear on the scene! May Jesus truly be glorified!

Tools for the Road

In closing, let me share with you quickly a few simple tools for the road. These will help ease your way as you learn and gain fluency in your own dream language.

1. Get around people who are further along than you are—people who dream and who talk about their dreams.

2. Study different materials from various authors.

3. Get a notebook for journaling and recording your insights on your dreams.

4. Get a little tape recorder and some tapes (15-minute tapes are fine) to use at times when journaling is inconvenient or impossible. This will help ensure that you can preserve your dream and your impressions until you have a chance to write them down.

5. Get understanding.

6. Get teaching.

7. Try to set your pre-bedtime routine so as to maximize quietness, resting, and listening.

8. Pray for impartation.

9. Finally, and most importantly, *love your Papa!*

Yes, these are a few tips from my journey of walking with the Lord in the night seasons. I have learned a lot since all of this began those many years ago. I trust that these dreams and lessons I have gleaned will inspire you on your journey and keep you going in the right direction!

Lean into your Beloved—He's waiting to give you a dream!

Reflection Questions

1. At the beginning of this chapter, Michal Ann tells us about a time she received an *actual dream* that appeared to be attended by angelic activity. How was this dream used in the ministry of worship?

2. What was one of her other dreams listed that encouraged you in your walk with God? How? Why?

3. According to Michal Ann, what are some of the practical tools for the road?

Referral Reading

Ethelbert W. Bullinger, *Numbers in Scripture* (Grand Rapids, MI: Kregel Publications, 1967).

James W. Goll, *Understanding Supernatural Encounters Study Guide* (Franklin, TN: Encounters Network, 2005).

▶ ▶ ▶ ▶ ▶ ▶
▶ ▶ ▶ ▶ ▶ ▶
▶ ▶ ▶ ▶ ▶ ▶
▶ ▶ ▶ ▶ ▶ ▶
▶ ▶ ▶ ▶ ▶ ▶
▶ ▶ ▶ ▶ ▶ ▶
▶ ▶ ▶ ▶ ▶ ▶
▶ ▶ ▶ ▶ ▶ ▶

CHAPTER TEN

JOURNALING AS A TOOL OF RETAINING REVELATION

Do need help retaining what you have already received? Then I have a simple remedy for you: Journal! Yes, it is another one of those awesome spiritual disciplines! Journaling is a tried and tested spiritual tool that will help you retain revelation and grow in your capacity to discern the voice of the Holy Spirit. Michal Ann and I have tried it, and it works!

Basically, journaling is simply a method of keeping notes for future reference. It can take many forms. Your journal may consist of your prayers, a record of God's answers as you perceive them, and/or a record of what you sense the Holy Spirit is saying to you through His various delivery systems. Journaling is a fundamental and clearly useful biblical discipline.

Some believers express concern that journaling is an attempt to put subjective revelation on the same level of authority as Scripture. This is not the case at all. The Bible *alone* is the infallible Word of God. Journaling is just another tool to help us retain and be more faithful with what He speaks to us.

God speaks to His children much of the time! However, we do not always differentiate His voice from our own thoughts, and thus we are timid at times about stepping out in faith. If we clearly learn to retain what He is speaking to us, we will know that He has already confirmed

His voice and Word to us. Thus we will be enabled to walk out God's words to us with greater confidence. Journaling then becomes a way of sorting out God's thoughts from our own.

As it has been for so many, the simple art of recording revelation may prove to be one of the missing links in your own walk of hearing God's voice. Continuity of language, divine suggestions and reminders, and also learning the proper interpretation of symbols will occur as you use journaling as a creative tool of storing up and later deciphering revelation.

I strongly encourage you to start journaling now if you have not already done so. The principles, tips, and suggestions in this chapter will help you get off to a strong start. Those of you who are already engaged in journaling, I urge you to continue!

To encourage you as to the value of journaling, let me share some thoughts on the subject from another elder friend, Herman Riffel. Herman is one of the "patriarchs" of modern-day visionary revelation—an authority not only on dreams and their interpretation but also on journaling as an effective method of retaining revelation.

In life we keep the treasures we value. Unwanted mail that comes is tossed away with just a glance. But bills, whether we like them or not, are carefully laid aside until we pay them. Checks are deposited in the bank so that no money is lost. Diplomas and certificates of recognition are hung on the wall for others to see.

What do we do with the promises the Lord gives us? They are worth more than any amount of money. What happens to the lessons we have learned through difficult and costly experiences? Too often we forget within a day or two the words of encouragement God gave us. The promises vanish away in the midst of new problems, unless we make a proper record of them.

I know by personal experience. Lillie and I pray for our children regularly, often for specific needs. Then we wait on the Lord for His answer, and graciously He gives us a word of encouragement.

Recently one of these words came to us: *Salvation shall spring forth like the grass and you will rejoice with joy unspeakable, for I will do what I have promised. Therefore, wait in patience and trust in Me, for I am faithful.*

This was an encouraging word and we did rejoice in it. Just a few days later, however, I asked Lillie if she remembered what the promise was that God had given. She did not remember, and neither did I, for problems had absorbed our attention again. Since I keep a journal, however, we were able to check it, find the promise, and again receive encouragement.[148]

Mr. Riffel also speaks to the practicality of journaling for spiritual growth and daily communion with God:

I urge you to begin keeping a journal, if you are not already doing so. What to include in a spiritual journal? One of the first things we may record in the day are our dreams, because they come before our work begins. We cannot determine the importance of a dream until we have seen the whole of it and listen to its message. We need to have pencil and paper handy, therefore, so that immediately upon awakening, before our minds begin to plan the activities of the day, we can catch the fleeting dream. As we work on the dream, we can record its interpretation and message for us.

Then we may record the Scripture through which God speaks to us that day. Since the journal is a record of our spiritual journeys, not simply a diary to record daily activities, the events of the day will provide the setting for the Lord's working. Therefore we listen to what God is saying to our hearts. To do that we meditate on the Scriptures, or we may sit in contemplation of our Lord Himself. We need to learn to "waste time with the Lord," from the world's viewpoint, in order to hear what God wants to say to us. We may then record any dialogue, or the result of the direction we have received.[149]

Discipline or Privilege?

Such is the principle of journaling. Obviously, there are many different forms of journaling. Our focus in this book is on journaling our dream language, but we can journal many other aspects of our Christian lives. There are prayer journals and daily devotional journals, for example. People keep different types of journals for different purposes.

Some people would describe journaling as a spiritual discipline. I prefer another term. Like many others, I have used the phrase "spiritual discipline" for years to describe any habitual practice we undertake to facilitate spiritual growth. When composing my book *The Lost Art of Practicing His Presence,* however, the Holy Spirit said to me, "You're not disciplined enough to have a spiritual discipline." That nailed me!

"Okay," I replied, surprised and a little miffed. (Deep in my heart, though, I knew He was right.)

He said, "These are spiritual privileges." That put a whole new angle on things. I really like the phrase, "spiritual privileges," because that is what they are. Looking at them as privileges rather than as disciplines completely changes your mind-set because doing something as a discipline can sometimes lead to a performance-based mentality. Doing the same thing as a privilege, however, means doing it because you can do it, because you see the value in doing it, because God enables you to do it, and because you want to do it—not because you have to do it to please God or stay on His "good side." It becomes a matter of perspective, like the difference between saying the glass is half empty or half full. Praying, studying, fasting, worshiping—they are all amazing spiritual privileges—with great benefits!

Lessons From Habakkuk and Daniel

Journaling our spiritual experiences has clear biblical precedent. Several times in the Book of Revelation, John is instructed to record what he sees. In fact, the entire Book of Revelation itself is a divinely inspired record of a series of awesome and incredible visions that John saw while *"in the Spirit on the Lord's day."*[150]

The discipline of spiritual journaling appears also in the Old Testament. Consider, for example, these words from the prophet Habakkuk:

> *I will stand on my guard post and station myself on the rampart; and I will keep watch to see what He will speak to me, and how I may reply when I am reproved. Then the Lord answered me and said, "Record the vision and inscribe it on tablets, that the one who reads it may run. For the vision is yet for the appointed time; it hastens toward the goal and it will not fail. Though it tarries, wait for it; for it will certainly come, it will not delay."*[151]

Habakkuk is seeking a spiritual experience. He is seeking to hear the *Rhema* voice of God directly in his heart so that he can understand what he sees around him. First of all, he goes to a quiet place where he can be alone and become still. Second, he quiets himself within by "watching to see" what God would say. Last of all, when God begins to speak, the first thing He says is, "Record the vision." Habakkuk wrote down what he was sensing in his heart. The benefits of this type of journaling were retained for years to come so that those who would later read it would be able to "run with it." Often the vision is fulfilled by others, so here we have another great benefit: If the revelation is preserved, then another group, city, or even generation can learn the lessons and move forward themselves.

Daniel was another biblical prophet who journaled. In fact, the seventh chapter of the Book of Daniel is essentially Daniel's journal entry regarding a significant and powerful dream:

> *In the first year of Belshazzar king of Babylon Daniel saw a dream and visions in his mind as he lay on his bed; then he wrote the dream down and related the following summary of it."*[152]

If you read Daniel's account of his dream in the rest of the chapter, you'll find that Daniel did not write down all the details of his amazing and rather intense dream. While in a spirit of rest, he composed a summary of his encounter. Too many people get caught up in the microscopic details in their sincere attempts at journaling and thus end up missing the primary emphasis of their visitation. Be like Daniel—write down a summary and keep it simple! The Holy Spirit will have a way of bringing back to your remembrance the details you might need later.

I take enormous encouragement from the life of Daniel. His style of journaling particularly appeals to me. Daniel's life spanned almost the entire 70-year period of the Babylonian exile. The events recorded in the Book of Daniel cover much of that same period of time, yet it is only 12 chapters long. Obviously, Daniel did not record everything he experienced; or, at least, not everything he recorded has survived to come down to us today. The Book of Daniel records the highlights, the most spiritually significant events in the life of Daniel and his people. A lifetime of experience is condensed into 12 short chapters—a summary, as it were.

When it comes to journaling, here's the bottom line: Do what works for you. I can give you plenty of practical tips, but in the end you have to decide what you feel most comfortable with. Perhaps you like to write and are good at it; you may prefer to record a full account of your dreams and experiences. However, if you lack the time or inclination to write long accounts, do what Daniel and other prophets did and write a summary. Set down the simplest, most basic sequence of events as a framework for recording in detail the highlights in the most salient or significant points. Whatever—make it simple, practical, and attainable.

Tips on Remembering Dreams

Some people tell me that they do not hear from God in their dreams—period! Others say they simply can't remember their dreams. Still others seem to remember only a fragment or portions of scattered images, which at the time do not seem to make much sense to them. But you were born to be a dreamer.

Sleep specialists tell us that everyone dreams for a period of time while in rapid eye movement (REM) sleep. So, in reality, all of us dream at some point every night. The issue then becomes one of knowing some practical tips and learning to rest under the anointing of the Holy Spirit in order to recall what we have been shown.

The Scriptures speak of the fleeting nature of dreams:

He flies away like a dream, and they cannot find him; even like a vision of the night he is chased away. [153]

Daniel 2:1-47 expresses the frustration that Nebuchadnezzar, the king of Babylon, experienced as he received a detailed dream but could not recall it! The dream disturbed the king so much that he searched for relief and health! God heard his plea and sent Daniel who, after a season of seeking the face of God, related to the king not only his dream itself but also its interpretation. In reality, of course, it was God who revealed these things to Daniel. Daniel sought God's face, and God gave him the spirit of understanding. If you seek God's face the way Daniel did, God will do the same for you.

Of course, no commitment to journaling will do any good if you cannot remember your dreams. You will remember that we discussed this problem and some possible solutions in detail in chapters three and four. At this point, however, I would like to add a few practical tips for retaining revelation. These steps will enhance your ability to journal effectively and enable you to remember your dreams longer.

1. If possible, get rid of your loud alarm clock. Ask the Holy Spirit to help you wake up. Try to establish the habit of getting up at a set time. This requires discipline and will naturally be harder for some than for others.

2. Many dreams come between four and five o'clock in the morning. Whenever you awaken, learn to linger for a few minutes in a place of rest, if possible.

3. Instead of an alarm, consider waking to a clock radio tuned to soothing music. This is what I did for years. I got rid of the blaring alarm and woke up to classical music, which doesn't chase away dreams. Classical music actually helps create a soothing atmosphere conducive to dream retention. Worship music has the same effect, particularly the softer, more soaking, reflective styles.

Be prepared to record your revelations by observing a few practical tips:

Keep a note pad and a pen by the bed so you won't have to get up before you record your dream. A simple spiral notebook works fine.

This is a personal journal. Grammar, neatness, and spelling are not critical issues. Content is crucial!

Consider using a small tape recorder. Michal Ann mentioned this in the last chapter. Keep it by your bedside so that all you have to do is turn over and whisper into it.

Later in the day or week, consider word processing the scribbles you previously captured. Some people transfer their experiences to a more permanent "journal." I keep both a personal dream journal and a ministry dream journal in my bag at all times!

Develop your dream alphabet by keeping track of symbols. Ask, "What does this symbol mean to me?" and "Can I find it in Scripture?"

Make note of your feelings/emotions in the dream/revelation. When you summarize your dream, be sure to describe how you felt during the dream, even if you include only a few words.

Be still and try to recall one or two of the details, and then your memory will kick in (see Zech. 4:1-2). Find one thread of the dream and then, in prayer, gently pull and more will appear on your screen.

Date all entries. This is important for many reasons, not the least of which is keeping track of patterns or progressions that may occur in your dream journey.

If traveling, record your location at the time of your dream. This can be just as important as the date. The locale may prove to be highly significant to interpreting your dream.

Expect God's love to be affirmed toward you. And then, as you receive it, expect the gifts of the Holy Spirit to be in operation.

Whenever possible, seek training and wise counsel from gifted interpreters of dreams. Not everyone will have this capacity as well developed as others. Even in Scripture, Daniel and Joseph are the only ones who are specifically mentioned as having this gift. Just as in the New Testament, we have the gift of speaking in tongues, but corresponding to it we have the gift of interpretation of tongues. Ask for the interpretation! You have not because you ask not!

Practical Applications in Quietness

One key principle in retaining revelation is to learn to be still before the Lord—to quiet our mind and spirit and wait on Him. It says in Psalms, *"Be still, and know that I am God."*[154] Years ago, the Holy Spirit taught me that stillness is the incubation bed of revelation. Quietness can actually be a form of faith because it is the opposite of anxiety and worry. Many times that is easier said than done. So, just how do you learn to become still before God?

I'll try to answer. First, remove external distractions. Mark 1:35 says that Jesus went to a secluded place to pray. Find a place where you can get away. For me, when I was growing up, I would get away by taking long walks. My family lived in a rural community in northwest Missouri. There were railroad tracks less than 300 yards from our house, and I used to get on those tracks and walk for miles. Hour after hour I would walk and talk to God. Outdoors and alone was the best place for me to have my communal time with the lover of my soul. Distractions were minimal. I could talk to God and listen to Him talk to me.

I have to fight for this alone time today. But whether it is a walk in the hills of Franklin, Tennessee, lingering in my bed with the covers pulled over my head, sitting in my special chair, or quieting my soul while listening to my favorite soaking CD, nothing takes the place of time alone with God!

Second, you must quiet your inner being. One of the biggest challenges in this will be your mind's tendency to suddenly remember all sorts of things that you need to do. The best way to counter that is by taking a few moments to write down all those things so that you can remember to do them later. Then, put them out of your head. Your mind should be at rest on those matters because you have taken action and not simply tried to ignore them. Release your personal tensions and anxieties to the Lord, *"casting all your anxiety on Him, because He cares for you."*[155] Finally, focus your meditating on the person of Jesus. Yes, focus on Jesus!

In becoming still, you are not trying to do anything. You simply want to be in touch with your Divine Lover, Jesus. Center on this moment of time and experience Him in it. All of these things will help you silence the inner noise of voices, thoughts, pressures, etc., that otherwise would force their way to the top. This grace of becoming still before God is often referred to as contemplative prayer.

Quietness has a great deal to do with your having a spirit of revelation in your life. Commit yourself to creating a spiritual culture where the Holy Dove will want to come and stay. Pull down the shades over the windows of your soul. Enter the Holy of Holies in your heart where Jesus the Messiah lives. Yes, He has taken up residence within you! He is there, and He is waiting to commune with you.

You are now a candidate to receive revelation! In some way, *Rhema* is couched in vision. The Book of Habakkuk opens with the words, *"The oracle* [or burden] *which Habakkuk the prophet saw."*[156] The prophet quieted himself to *watch* and see what the Lord would speak. As we have seen, focusing the eyes of our heart upon God causes us to become inwardly still. It raises our level of faith and expectancy and results in our being more fully open to receive from God.

Wisdom Ways With Journaling

Any venture into new territory is fraught with perils and pitfalls; receiving and retaining revelation is no different. Here are some practical safeguards to help protect you as you embark on your adventure.

1. Cultivate a humble, teachable spirit. Never allow the attitude, "God told me, and that's all there is to it." All revelation is to be tested. You will make mistakes. Accept that as a part of the learning process and go on.

2. Have a good working knowledge of the Bible. Remember, *Rhema* is based on *Logos*. The revelatory never conflicts with the written Word!

3. God primarily gives revelation for the area in which He has given responsibility and authority. *Look for revelation in areas of your responsibility.* Stay away from ego trips that motivate you to seek revelation for areas in which God has not yet placed you.

4. Walk together with others. Realize that until your guidance is confirmed, it should be regarded as what you *think* God is saying.

5. Realize that if you submit to God and resist the devil, he *must* flee from you! You can trust the guidance of the Holy Spirit to lead you into truth.

Add this tool of journaling to your "tool box" and you will mature in the grace of retaining revelation and the capacity of discerning God's voice. As you get ready to begin, you may wish to pray a prayer like this one:

"Father, grant me the grace to journal, in Jesus' great name. Teach me the skills of how to retain revelation and clearly discern the flow of Your voice. Lead me in Your wisdom applications of recording what You reveal. In Jesus' wonderful name, Amen."

Now, let's just do it! Experience is always the best teacher!

Reflection Questions

1. What are some of the practical tips to help you retain revelation?

2. What are some of the ways that you can quiet your soul in order to hear from the Lord?

3. In the closing of the chapter, James lists some wisdom ways for journaling. What are a couple of these that you feel you could incorporate into your own life?

Referral Reading

Mark and Patti Virkler, *Communion With God* (Shippensburg, PA: Destiny Image, 1990).

Walter Wilson, *Wilson's Dictionary of Bible Types* (Grand Rapids, MI: William B. Eerdman's Publishing Company, 1950).

James W. Goll, *The Lost Art of Practicing His Presence* (Shippensburg, PA: Destiny Image, 2006).

CHAPTER ELEVEN

WHEN GOD
SEEMS SILENT

I have often said that dry seasons are times when character is formed, while wet seasons are times of growth when gifts are given and developed. Have you ever had a dry season? A season when God seemed silent? A season when you received no revelation? A season when your prayers appeared to go unanswered?

If you have walked the road of discipleship with Christ for very long at all, I am sure you already know what I mean when I talk about a dry season. If you are a Christian and have never experienced a dry season, you will at some point. Guaranteed! A dry season is not much fun when you are going through it, but it is essential for strong spiritual growth.

Wet seasons are times of blessing, times of growth and expansion, of fruitfulness and promotion. Dry seasons are seasons of pruning and preparation in anticipation of the next wet season. Dry seasons are the times of the cross, and wet seasons are the times of resurrection life. In order to build healthy, balanced Christian lives we need both.

It is one thing to know that dry seasons will come but quite another to know what to do when they arrive. What do you do when God seems silent? How do you cope when your channel of revelation and words from the Lord seems to have dried up? Quite often when this happens you will be tempted to quit, to give up. That is the last thing you should do! A dry season is a time to press in to the Lord harder and farther and with more passion than before. In fact, that is one of God's primary reasons for letting us go through periods of dryness—to make us thirstier for Him.

My Personal Acquaintance With Silence

My initiation into silence began quite early. The rural United Methodist church where I grew up had a balcony loft area where you could peer down upon the main sanctuary. I was a singer from a young age, often positioned in the loft patiently looking down on the congregation, as the pianist, organist, and pastor on the platform would perform opening rituals.

Many times I was the one who actually began the service. Standing in the darkened loft all alone with no instrument or pitch pipe, I would sing with my melodic high-pitched voice, "The Lord is in His holy temple; let all the earth keep silent before Him." And then the service would proceed. I sang that Sunday after Sunday until I hit the age in life called puberty—and my voice began to change. I still remember the Sunday I quit, the day I sang high and then suddenly low in one phrase. I was so embarrassed that I did not come down from the balcony that day, but stayed up in the loft. I needed some personal self-imposed *sozo* (healing) time. That Sunday I received one of my first lessons in silence. There is a test that always comes with silence.

Years later, when I entered into a traveling ministry, I traveled all over the United States and North America and visited several other countries, releasing prophetic words to people everywhere I went. Only the Lord knows how many prophetic words of encouragement I spoke to individuals, congregations, leaders, cities, and nations, but it seemed as though it was in the thousands.

Yet in all that time, during all those years of releasing public prophetic words to others, I rarely, if ever, received a public prophetic word myself. I had received private prophetic words, but no one of recognition had ever spoken a confirming word over me in a public setting.

But the real problem for me, which was really painful personally, was the fact that all my ministerial buddies were getting three and four prophetic words, public affirmations, direction, etc.—and I was not. It seemed like everybody was getting extraordinary words except for me. And that hurt. I did not understand it. My security was being tested and I was manifesting!

For me, God seemed silent.

Michal Ann and I are no strangers to the periodic seasons some have called the "dark night of the soul." God does speak. He has spoken to us many times in the past, and I am convinced that He will continue to speak to us in the future. But I would be lying if I did not admit to you that some of the things we have been through as a family made it seem as though God was silent. Where was His miracle work? Where was His hedge of protection? Where was the God of supernatural encounters? Where was God when I needed Him? We have experienced days and even weeks—shall I be even more honest and say *months*—when God seemed silent.

The word "seemed" is very important here. God may seem silent at times, but He is always active. God is always at work. Yet He does not always tell us what He is doing at the time. All we can do is recall His past faithfulness in speaking to us and trust that He will do so again according to His own timetable.

He Did Not Answer Her a Word

Personal experience is not valid unless it can be backed up from the Word of God. With that in mind, let's turn to the Scriptures for some insight on this matter of the silence of God. In my own educational background as a social worker, I read the Bible at times from out of my educational paradigm. What I mean is that I read the biblical accounts as true-life events, but I also ask God to help me go beyond the print on the page—to help me dive into the stories, to show me how the people felt, to capture some of the feeling and flavor of what it was like actually to be there. That is what we will try to do here.

Let's begin with Matthew's account of Jesus' encounter with a Canaanite woman.

> *Jesus...withdrew into the district of Tyre and Sidon. And a Canaanite woman from that region came out and began to cry out, saying, "Have mercy on me, Lord, Son of David; my daughter is cruelly demon-possessed." But He did not answer her a word. And His disciples came and implored Him, saying, "Send her away, because she keeps shouting at us." But He answered and said, "I was sent only to the lost sheep of the house of Israel."*[157]

Try to imagine this scene. Jesus has left Jerusalem with His disciples and withdrawn into the district of Tyre and Sidon—a Gentile region—possibly for a time of rest and rejuvenation. Suddenly, a Canaanite woman comes up and pleads with Jesus to heal her demon-possessed daughter. And Jesus says…*nothing*. Dive into the heart of this woman. Put yourself in her place. As a Gentile, she probably did not even worship the same God as Jesus and His disciples. As a pagan, she may very well have been involved in occultic religious practices. The fact that her daughter was demonized suggests a problem with generational iniquities and generational curses. As a mother, she is desperate to find a way to help her daughter.

Somewhere she has heard about a man named Jesus who can perform miracles, and when she learns that Jesus is in her district, she wastes no time in pursuing Him. She already has some knowledge of who He is because she addresses Him as "Jesus, Son of David." The woman is also discerning enough to know the true nature of her daughter's problem.

When she finds Jesus, she pleads for His help; but He remains silent. To make matters worse, Jesus' disciples, annoyed by the woman's loud pleading, urge Jesus to send her away.

They were probably embarrassed because they did not yet have the authority to deal with this problem, and she was "hot-dogging" them. This woman is relentless. She will not let go of this thing, and her shouting and loud pleading grow more obnoxious by the minute. (She may have had a religious spirit, feeling that somehow she had to persuade Jesus to help her. After all, that was what she had to do to get the attention of the gods in her own religion.)

Matthew does not tell us how long this went on. It must have lasted at least several minutes; at least long enough for the disciples to become thoroughly annoyed.

Imagine it: This woman is shouting and pleading and getting louder by the minute. The disciples are standing there, shuffling their feet and hanging their heads or looking around nervously to see who else might be witness to this spectacle. All the while Jesus is sitting there passive and silent.

We know, of course, that Jesus eventually grants the woman's request and heals her daughter. The issue we are concerned with here is His silence. He did not immediately answer her. For a time, this poor, desperate woman had no idea whether or not Jesus was going to respond. Would He ignore her? Would He send her away as His disciples wanted? Or would He answer her plea? She didn't have a clue. All she had was hope.

Have you ever been in a similar situation? Has there ever been a time when you felt your whole world was coming apart at the seams and you prayed and pleaded and yet God seemed silent? If so, then you know how frightening and discouraging such a time can be. My hope and prayer for you is that after reading this chapter you will look at the dry seasons of your life from a different perspective. Remember that God loves you and has your very best at heart. Trust Him and He will help you learn to view your dry seasons redemptively and even come to see them as friends.

Handling the "Why?" Question

A noted philosopher once said that a man can live with his existence if he has a *why* for his existence. You can make it through almost anything if you know why. Jesus was given fully to the issue of why. The day came when even Jesus Himself had a dry season. Throughout eternity, from ages past and even through His time on earth in human flesh, the Son of God had enjoyed unbroken fellowship with His Father. Never had Jesus known the silence of His Father—until He went to the cross.

As all the sin of mankind from every generation past, present, and future came crashing down on Jesus' shoulders at Calvary, He felt His Father turn His face away, and then Jesus experienced the greatest loneliness anyone has ever known. In anguish He cried out, *"My God, My God, why have You forsaken Me?"*[158] From Heaven came a deafening silence. As far as we know from Scripture, Jesus never received an answer.

I think it is rather ironic that the very God who allows us to experience dry seasons knows Himself exactly how it feels to go through such a time. At the same time, I draw comfort and encouragement from that fact. Jesus knows how we feel when God seems silent. And He can help us get through it.

Handling the "How?" and "When?" Questions

Another encounter from the life of Jesus provides additional insight into the question of the seeming silence of God. This time John is the narrator.

After these things there was a feast of the Jews, and Jesus went up to Jerusalem. Now there is in Jerusalem by the sheep gate a pool, which is called in Hebrew Bethesda, having five porticoes. In these lay a multitude of those who were sick, blind, lame, and withered, [waiting for the moving of the waters; for an angel of the Lord went down at certain seasons into the pool and stirred up the water; whoever then first, after the stirring up of the water, stepped in was made well from whatever disease with which he was afflicted.] A man was there who had been ill for thirty-eight years. When Jesus saw him lying there, and knew that he had already been a long time in that condition, He said to him, "Do you wish to get well?" The sick man answered Him, "Sir, I have no man to put me into the pool when the water is stirred up, but while I am coming, another steps down before me." Jesus said to him, "Get up, pick up your pallet and walk." Immediately the man became well, and picked up his pallet and began to walk. Now it was the Sabbath on that day. [159]

Jesus identifies with us and answers the "why" question. At times, though, we also face the "when" question, as God seems silent. From John's account we know that the crippled man who met Jesus at the pool of Bethesda was healed miraculously that day. But what about the 38 years that preceded it? Where was God then? Let's try to put ourselves in the place of this crippled man, not out of pity but out of reality and understanding.

John says that the crippled man had been in this condition for 38 years. We have to remember that in those days medicine was still in a very primitive state. Little or no provision was made for health care or the needs of invalids. There were no wheelchairs or handicap ramps. Unless family members took care of them, lame persons such as he usually were reduced to begging in order to survive. Every day for 38 years he had lain by the pool of Bethesda, waiting for the stirring of the waters. Perhaps the man had no family. I wonder how many days and times he lay there in his own urine just wanting help. He probably reached the place many times of just wanting to give up. At any rate, he had no one to help him into the pool when the water was stirred and he was unable to get in by himself, so someone else always got in ahead of him and he would miss his chance. It was a pretty hopeless situation.

Why did he persist? Why did he stay there day after day? Perhaps he had nowhere else to go. This man apparently possessed at least a measure of faith. He believed in the stirring of the waters. He believed that an angel from God occasionally stirred the water so that the first person to enter the pool would be healed. Perhaps he stayed there day after day because he always held out a glimmer of hope that one day it would be his day.

How did this man get to the pool? Perhaps he lived there. Maybe he had staked out his own little corner under one of the porticoes so he would be safe from the sun and the rain. More likely, however, is that someone brought him. Many miracles require two elements: a man or a woman and a supernatural God. God then uses that man or woman as a conduit for His wonder-working power. You may be the man or woman whom God wants to use in just such a manner.

One day Jesus came to the pool. With all the multitudes of sick and desperate people who undoubtedly were at the pool, why did Jesus single out this man? The Bible does not say. Imagine the scene: scores, perhaps hundreds, of sick people with all sorts of ailments crowded together as close to the water as possible. Some are moaning, some are screaming from pain, some are weeping, some are cursing, and some are praying. Many others simply sit or lie in silence with hopelessness in their eyes. On everyone's mind are the questions: "When will the angel come? How will I get in? Will I get in first? Will today be my healing day?"

Jesus asks the crippled man, "Do you want to get well?" The man's response comes, in part, from out of his fatigue factor after years of disappointment: "I have no man to put me into the pool." Jesus shows up in the middle of the why, the how, and the when and asks the man a rather bizarre question. He is saying, in effect, "Hey you, lying there on that pallet, why are you here anyway? What is it you really want?"

What Do You Do?

Have you ever wondered how this crippled man felt when time after time he saw others get into the pool and get healed but it never happened for him? What do you suppose he did when others got in and were healed? Did he rejoice with them? Or did he sink into a sullen mood of bitterness and envy?

Let's bring this up close and personal. What do *you* do when someone receives a blessing or a healing and you do not? How do you respond when someone else receives a powerful dream or some awesome revelation and you do not? Do you rejoice with them? Or do you burn with envy and wonder why God seems to be silent in your case? What does someone else's success or good favor do for your faith? How do you handle it when somebody else gets the dream that you feel you needed and you get nothing? Do you take it in stride or do you fret and fuss and say, "When is it my turn?"

Please hear me: God is good all the time! In His fatherly graciousness He answers many of our questions immediately. He blesses us and imparts gifts and revelation and dreams and visions to us. But sometimes He chooses to be silent. When He does, that is when we must look past the outward and deep into our heart. When everyone around us is getting touched, healed, and renewed, or is receiving revelation and we are not, we need to ask, "Why am I still here? What am I after anyway?"

Why did that crippled man stay at the pool of Bethesda every day? He probably could have gotten someone to take him away or simply stopped coming. But he didn't. Perhaps, despite years of disappointment, he still believed. He still held out hope that his day would come. What are you going to do when God seems silent and the dreams do not come or their promised fulfillment appears to be delayed? Are you going to give up and say, "I guess this just isn't for me"? Or are you going to stay by the pool and wait for God to stir the waters?

Why are you still here? What keeps you coming back? Is it because somewhere, somehow, you caught a glimpse of the unshakable Kingdom of God that is being established in the earth? There is a Kingdom that will stand even when the earth itself is shaken! Hold fast to that belief because it is in these times of waiting, when God seems silent, that the enemy will come and say, "Well, you don't deserve revelation anyway."

Guess what? In one sense, you don't. None of us do. God gives us revelation because of His grace and favor, not because of our merit or performance. But then there is the other side to this: If you are truly "born again," then you are a son or daughter of the Father. Every pauper gets turned into a prince in this great Kingdom. It's all available through grace and faith in the Lord Jesus Christ. Yes, God is good all the time, and His mercies endure forever!

Unless you know why you keep coming back, other thoughts will eat at you: "God apparently does not want to endorse me. That is why I am not receiving anything"; or "Does God even know where I live?"

Eventually, the frustration level can get so high that you will be tempted to throw in the towel: "Forget you guys! Hang it up!"

Don't let this happen to you. What you need is a little heavenly perspective.

Perspective in the Midst of the Valley

Why isn't God speaking? Why is there a withholding of revelation? Have you ever asked those questions? I know in my insecurity and immaturity I have.

Years ago in Kansas City, I had the privilege of being exposed to realms of the prophetic that were absolutely profound. The seers of the seers, the statesmen of the statesmen, the dreamers of the dreams, the prophetic teachers of the prophetic teachers, the prophetic intercessors of the prophetic intercessors—we were all in a strange collegiality together, and people came from all over the world to look in our goldfish bowl to see who we were. It was awesome on one hand and a lot of pressure on the other.

I was younger and gifted and less secure in my identity in Christ. And I did not get the confirmation that I thought I deserved. As I mentioned earlier, for years I did not receive a single personal public word from one of these recognized prophets. I *gave* words and revelation to many but never once *got* a public prophetic word myself. (By the way, our identity is not who we get a word from either! Have I ever had some growing up to do!)

Is it any surprise, then, that I began asking the "why" and the "how" and the "when" questions? From my perspective, compared to all those I was walking with at that time, God seemed silent. *I too am in transition,* I thought. *Why them and not me? I too have needs.* On and on my sad list of comparisons went.

Why wasn't God speaking? Why was there a withholding of revelation? As I searched out these questions, several possible answers emerged. First, I might be relying too much on an external witness rather than on the internal witness of the Holy Spirit in my heart. Second, perhaps it wasn't a *kairos* moment yet; the strategic timing had not yet come. Third, maybe my expectations were off base. If your expectations are misplaced, too high or off base, you are sure to end up disappointed. Fourth, perhaps I was chasing for words from men instead of the Word Himself. People will fail, and their words will fail, but He who is the Word will never fail. Finally, there was the possibility of spiritual warfare and/or a deaf and dumb spirit hindering mine and others' ability to hear, speak, release, and receive.

I never did get a public release of affirmation until I resolved these internal issues. But I had to reach a personal crisis point. It came to the place where Michal Ann and I had gotten tired of the circus that seemed to surround some of the great gatherings. Frustrated over the whole business, I remember saying, "Lord, I don't need to play this game any more. You are my source!" Did I still care? Yes. Did I still have needs? Yes. But I was finished with chasing men for words. And that is when things began to change.

Responses to Dry Seasons

So how do you get through a dry season? When God seems silent, there are several things you can do.

1. Stick with what you already know. What was the last thing the Lord said to you or told you to do? Have you done it? Why should He tell you something new until you have completed what He has already revealed?

2. God may be testing you. What do you believe?

3. Don't doubt in darkness what you have seen or heard in times of light.

4. Don't compare yourself with others. This is one of the biggest ditches to avoid. Just because God works a certain way with someone else does not mean He will work the same way with you. God will work with you in a way that is significantly personal to you.

5. Be childlike. Don't be overly complicated! Hold out your hand, take hold of His, and say, "Daddy."

6. Don't expect everything to be so dramatic! Don't be a prophetic junkie, so addicted to the external that you lose your way concerning the ways of God with revelation. Are you addicted to the Word of God, the Man of the Word? There are

withdrawal seasons, and they are purposeful because God wants to make sure that you are anchored in Him.

7. How about the person sitting next to you? Can God speak through him/her? Could it be that you are looking for the revelation or the dream or whatever to come in a certain package in a certain way? Could it be that God wants to use one of His little princes or children to speak a word of encouragement, exhortation, or comfort to you?

8. Walk by faith and not by sight. Sometimes going from word to word is walking by sight and not by faith. Stick to the Word! Obey the Word!

9. Learn the wisdom lessons of true guidance.

Let me elaborate a little on this last one. Imagine that you are on the rooftop of a tall building watching a parade pass on the street below. From your vantage point you can see the beginning and end of the parade as well as everything in between. There are times in our lives when we are given a dream or a vision or some other type of revelation that allows us to have a "rooftop view," usually in sequences and stages, where we see the beginning and the middle and catch a glimpse of the end.

Most of the time, however, most of us live at ground level and have to look at life through a knothole on the fence. We can only see a tiny portion at any one time. We get a little peek and build our life on it as if that peek is the full picture. Then someone comes and stands in front of the knothole, and we can't see anything. The way we are accustomed to receiving revelation is blocked. All of a sudden, God seems silent. The parade is still there. Nothing has changed. We just cannot see it at the moment—but God can. This is how He chooses to work many times to teach us lessons in guidance. The rooftop perspective is the exception; the knothole view is the norm. We have to understand that guidance and revelation come over a lifetime.

God's Purposes in Times of Silence

When God seems silent you must be faithful and keep pressing on through. This is what the Canaanite woman did who had the demonized daughter. She had pled with Jesus to heal her daughter, but Jesus had remained silent. Finally, when He did speak, Jesus told her that He had been sent only to the lost sheep of Israel. This was not what the woman wanted to hear, yet she refused to give up:

> But she came and began to bow down before Him, saying, "Lord, help me!" And He answered and said, "It is not good to take the children's bread and throw it to the dogs." But she said, "Yes, Lord; but even the dogs feed on the crumbs which fall from their masters' table." Then Jesus said to her, "O woman, your faith is great; it shall be done for you as you wish." And her daughter was healed at once.[160]

How did this woman respond when she was offended? What did she do when she did not receive the answer she had hoped for? She bowed low in worship. The word "worship" literally means to prostrate yourself. This woman prostrated herself before Jesus. She bowed low and, in the midst of a time when God seemed very silent, she worshiped.

We should do the same. When God seems silent—worship Him.

As she worshiped, the Canaanite woman received an invitation into greater union with God. Out of her worship came a revelation of dependency; she knew that Jesus was her only hope. In that knowledge and from the posture of worship she cried out, "Lord, help me!" Now this had become more than just intercession for her daughter. The woman saw her own condition and understood perhaps that her own condition was a key to her daughter's healing. She prostrated herself. No clenched fist, no attitude of self-righteousness, no pretentiousness, no posturing—she simply pleaded for help.

When God seems silent, remember that you are totally dependent on Him—even when He is silent.

Jesus' next words to the woman only seemed to make her situation worse. He said, in effect, "Do you really think I am going to give My children's bread to the dogs?" What an insult! (Keep in mind that all this time Jesus is testing the woman's heart.) To her everlasting credit, the woman did not arise to the provocation. She simply stated that even the dogs could eat the crumbs that fell from their master's table. In other words, she said, "Just let me have the crumbs and that will be enough." This woman was not going to be provoked. She kept her heart clean, even as Jesus' "insults" got worse.

When God seems silent, keep your heart clean because more opportunities for offenses will come!

Jesus offended the woman's mind in order to open her heart. Rather than simply heal her daughter, Jesus gave her the invitation to a greater union and to a greater cleansing.

When God seems silent, remember that sometimes He will offend your mind in order to reveal your heart.

This woman responded to Jesus' apparent rebuffs with incredible tenaciousness. Like Jacob wrestling with the angel, she would not let go until she received her blessing. Follow her example. If God seems silent, don't give up. Above all, do not let go of the Word of God and the God of the Word. Hang on for dear life, and in the end you will find that He has been with you all along.

When God seems silent, be tenacious! Do not let go!

This Canaanite woman pressed forward and received her inheritance. She got all she asked for and more. What if she had stopped along the way and decided it was useless to continue? She would have gone away empty-handed.

When God seems silent, keep going, regardless. Press forward and receive your inheritance.

With your inheritance in hand, rejoice and know that your victory is another person's test. Just as you once looked with envy on others who were receiving from God while you were not, someone else who is now going through a dark night of the soul will look on you the same way. Remember from whence you have come, and pray for that other person. Pray that he or she will soon discover what you now know from experience: No matter how dark the night, God is on the other side. And even though you may not be able to see Him, He is with you also in the midst of that dark night.

God Is on the Other Side!

Remember that your dry season is God's way of building your character. It is His way of preparing you for bigger and greater things. He has promised that He will never leave you or forsake you. When God seems silent, believe that He guides you even from His silence. Review your history. Remind yourself that God has guided you in the past. Tell yourself that God is guiding you now, in the present, and that He will guide you in the future.

Learn to be sensitive to others. Create within yourself a capacity for compassion. Realize that God is more than a jukebox machine where you drop in a quarter, push a button, and get Him to play your favorite tune. God is much bigger than that. He is more than a methodology. He is more than just a tool. He is more than just a gift giver. He is God Almighty—and you are not.

Learn how to hear God for yourself. Let me give you another lesson from life's journey with my friend the Holy Spirit. I used to do a lot of counseling. For a number of years I was a pastor. I really loved God and I really loved people. There was a spirit of counsel on my life. People would come in with a problem, and at times I would give them an answer. This went on for quite some time until one day the Holy Spirit spoke to me. I saw an image of a spoon, and the Spirit said, "Stop putting the spoon in their mouth. Teach them by putting it in their hand." In other words, I needed to help them learn how to hear God for themselves.

When God seems silent, it may be because you are trying to hear Him through others when He wants you to hear Him for yourself. "Trust Me!" says the Lord. "I am your Father." Good fathers speak to their children directly, and God is a good Father.

Learn to identify with Jesus on the cross. In Christ we have a Man who has gone through so much that we can fully identify with Him just as He has fully identified with us. Give yourself to Him and love Him with all your heart.

Finally, when God seems silent, recognize this as His invitation to you to come into greater union with Christ. God's silence is His way of calling you to press in. It is a strategic chess move on His part. "And now," He says, "it's your move." Press in, because silence is God's invitation to greater union with Him. When your dreams seem to fade away, press in because the God of dreams has not faded away. He is there waiting to embrace you and to expand your heart's capacity to receive more of His Word, His will, and His ways.

When God seems silent, *press in!*

Reflection Questions

1. When did Jesus experience a time when His Father appeared to be silent?

2. What lessons can you learn from the man who waited 38 years for the stirring of the waters at the pool of Bethesda?

3. What should you do when you experience a dry season or when God seems silent in your own life?

Referral Reading

Iverna Thompkins with Judson Cornwall, *On the Ash Heap With No Answers* (Altamonte Springs, CA: Creation House, 1992).

James W. Goll, *Consecrated Contemplative Prayer* (Franklin, TN: Encounters Network, 2005).

CHAPTER TWELVE

HANDLING DREAMS WITH WISDOM

Revelation is hot stuff! Like a pot of boiling water on a stove, it can burn you if you mishandle it. Always put on your "mittens" of wisdom before trying to carry your cargo of revelation to its place of usefulness and purpose. Otherwise, it might spill on you!

Sometimes we get so caught up in seeking revelation that we never stop to consider how we will handle it after it comes. Revelation in the hands of an immature or unprepared vessel can be a dangerous thing! Too many precious believers have been hurt, misled, or discouraged by mishandled revelation. That is why God is so careful about the *whom* and the *when* in imparting revelatory insight.

Your first step after receiving revelation should *always* be to call forth God's wisdom administration. If you do not, you will almost certainly mismanage your dream and end up burning yourself and others, rather than bringing healing and empowerment. Remember the scriptural proverb: *"A man will be praised according to his insight."*[161] Ask for God's insight with wisdom and understanding, and He will grant it.

Wisdom Applications for Beginners

Inexperience and overzealous application are two of the biggest pitfalls for well-intentioned beginners in the realm of dreams and dream interpretation. Those and other common mistakes can be avoided, or at least minimized, by applying some simple wisdom tips to your approach. Even if you are not a novice in the dream realm, it still never hurts to review the basics from time to time.

1. When interpreting a dream and presenting it to others, *turn your thoughts into a question.* "Does this mean anything to you?" Do not presume that you have all the information or that you already know what the dream means for the other person. Ask the question of the other person to confirm or deny your impression. This is the safe route, especially when you are just starting out. It is also the path of humility.

2. *Turn your dream into intercession.* Pray the inspiration instead of sweating out the bullets of heavy perspiration! If you are interpreting, teach the other person how to pray the revelation. But *always* pray through your dream *before* you ever try to interpret it for someone else.

3. *Submit your revelation to trusted counsel* (and even a council). God will not give it all to you. Trust Him to speak through others as well.

4. Realize that *if you have received the genuine article, there will be some tension* that you'll have to walk through. "Do I sit on this, or do I run with it?" This tension is normal and is part of your learning curve.

5. Eventually, *another test will come.* You will be praised (elevated) because of your (really *His*) gift. What will you do with these trophies? Years ago, Bob Mumford, a prophetic statesman and teacher, said, "At the end of the day, I present my trophies to the Lord and I worship Him with them." That is wise counsel.

6. Learn the lesson quickly and well, as paraphrased from Proverbs 29:11: "*A fool opens wide his mouth and says all he knows.*" Ask the Holy Spirit questions. Watch and learn from others. "What should I say? To whom do I give it? When do I release it? Where do I present it?" Most of us learn this proverb by mistake and by the great tutor of experience! In the beginning, be sparing with what you present. Give it out in small portions to check out the receptivity. Don't show off or

forge blindly ahead and give out the whole revelation at once. Depending on the response, you may need to release another portion. Or you may find that you need to spend more time in prayer over the revelation before you release any more of it. It is a learning process.

Additional Application Tips

Once you begin moving in the realm of dreams and dream language you probably will hear at some point the phrase, "second-heaven revelation." Perhaps you have encountered the term already and wondered what it meant. The Bible speaks of a *"midheaven"*[162] and a *"third heaven,"*[163] implying the existence of a "first heaven." The first heaven is the sky above us, including space and all it contains. The second heaven is where the demonic realm is set up. And the third Heaven is God's dwelling place.

So what is "second-heaven revelation"? Different groups and individuals use different terms for this concept. Not everything you receive is a declaration of what is supposed to come to pass. It is possible that the Holy Spirit could give you insight into one of satan's schemes or plans. (Paul said that we are not to be ignorant of the devil's schemes.) Thus the term "second-heaven revelation" is sometimes used to refer to that information that is derived from the enemy's camp and used to enlighten us so as to prepare us for what is coming or, through intercession and/or spiritual warfare, cut it off from occurring.

Sometimes the Holy Spirit will retrieve information from the second heaven about satan's plan and then give it to you in a dream or vision. He is tipping you off about the enemy's intentions so you can take action in intercession or spiritual warfare. That is why solid interpretive skills and wisdom application are needed for discerning the meaning of such a dream.

Another practical wisdom way in handling revelation is to learn to *give your revelation with gentleness.* This is especially important if you have to deliver a warning. It is on this one point that many people trip up and make enormous mistakes. No matter how urgent the message seems to you, don't blunder in like a bull in a china shop. There is a process of "delivering the goods" in a manner in which they will be received. Go through the standard procedures of first *speaking*, second *exhorting,* and third *warning* with all authority. This is according to the pattern of Titus 2:15.[164]

Wisdom shouts the fear of the Lord. *"The fear of the Lord is the beginning of wisdom, and the knowledge of the Holy One is understanding."*[165] *Never* use your revelation as a tool of punishment! The Holy Spirit spoke to me once, "Be careful not to stretch the rod of your mouth out against the house that the Lord builds."

Another danger to avoid is allowing your ministry and reputation to be destroyed by false or misapplied revelation. You can become tainted by an evil report about a person, a church, or a ministry given to you by someone else under the guise of revelation. Take a lesson from Numbers chapters 13 and 14 where the Israelites listened to the negative report of the ten spies rather than the positive report of the two other spies, Joshua and Caleb, and therefore never fulfilled their destiny. Let the blood of Jesus wash you clean from the defilement of gossip and evil reports.

Finally, always be alert to the activity of the accuser of the brethren. He tries to spew filthy inspiration on believers.[166] "Be of sober spirit, be on the alert. Your adversary, the devil, prowls around like a roaring lion, seeking someone to devour."[167] Bart Druckenmiller, in his book *Dreams in the Spirit, Volume Two,* says it this way:

> It is very easy to misinterpret people's actions, motives, or intentions as well as all types of things especially in dreams. You may find yourself having a dream about a character flaw in someone else's life, and think the problem is with them, when God is really trying to show you something of that in your own life....
>
> Here is an important principle in dream interpretation: If the dream contradicts what you already know to be true, hold on to what you know to be true, and not the dream....
>
> We must quit shooting our wounded, which is what the accuser does....We don't need to help him.[168]

Responding to Your Dreams

Success and growth in the realm of dream language depends on learning the proper way to respond to your dreams. There is a simple three-stage process to follow when handling revelation of all types: revelation, interpretation, and application. God gives the revelation, but if you miss the interpretation, the application is doomed to failure! So, always seek God's Word, His will, and His ways when handling dreams.[169]

In addition to the simple three-stage process, there is also a series of simple steps for you to consider when responding to your dreams:[170]

1. Allow peace to rule in your mind and your heart at all times.

2. Write out a summary of your dream and date it.

3. Pray over the events and the circumstances of your dream, its content, and how it came to you.

4. At times, seek wise confidential counsel on how to proceed. And make sure it is someone who knows how to keep his/her mouth shut!

5. Consider seeking interpretation through others who are not involved in the situation. This helps ensure objectivity.

6. Do not act on your dream until its interpretation is confirmed. Seek confirmation at *all* times. Remember, God always confirms His Word by more than one witness. Don't sell your house and move to Peru on the strength of one dream! Get confirmation! Your spouse and your children will appreciate it!

7. When your dream's meaning has been confirmed, take only first steps toward its fulfillment. This is particularly true when dealing with "calling dreams."

8. Always remember that dreams are what your prophetic potential is—not automatic declarations of what will be!

9. Dreams almost always lead to a process of becoming. "An appropriate interpretation should bring you closer to God. The journey is as important as the destination to God. He measures maturity and character, but the dreamer may be more time conscious of progress as a measure of time. The process took Joseph 17 years to fulfill, but it was worth all the waiting."[171]

10. A dream may not always be logical! In fact, most dreams are *not* logical. But hang on to them and treasure them in your heart.

11. Plant the dreams in your heart and spirit and always remember: If it is from God, it is worth a good fight! Wage war with the promise when the circumstances seem to run contrary to your dream. Do not give up on your dreams!

Testing Your Dreams

One important step to responding to your dreams is learning to test the revelation to make sure it is true and valid. Here are some tips to help you build your discernment in this area:

Does the dream seem to contradict God's nature of being a good and loving Father who desires the best for each of His kids?

Does the dream contradict the principles of the written Word of God?

Does the dream glorify Jesus Christ and point people to Him and His work on the cross?

Does the dream build up your faith and cause you to desire a closer walk with the Lover of your soul?

Does the dream produce freedom in the grace of God or does it bring you and others into bondage and legalism?

Does the dream line up with God's overall plan for your life as you currently understand it? Does it seem to be a progression of what has already been revealed?

Does the dream cause you to move towards fellowship with the Body of Christ or does it create alienation and disorientation?

The Wisdom Model From Daniel's Life

Several years ago I had a dream in which I saw an old wooden box. Opening the lid, I saw an ancient parchment manuscript inside. It was the Book of Daniel. I sensed that the Holy Spirit was indicating to me that He was going to be opening up human minds with wisdom and revelation to fully understand the writings of the Book of Daniel.

Daniel himself wrote that his book was sealed up, to be unsealed at *"the end of time."*[172] I believe that the spirit of revelation is resting on the Book of Daniel and it is being opened up to us in these days.

The necessity of wisdom-filled and godly dream interpreters is greatly needed today. But as the end of the age unfolds, ambassadors of revelation with humble and accurate presentation will be needed all the more. Therefore, let us seek the Lord for a Daniel-type model to be restored.

The Book of Daniel provides an excellent pattern for us to follow. We will gain much insight into the wisdom ways of handling dreams by taking a close look at the dreams of King Nebuchadnezzar and the process through which Daniel interpreted them.[173]

Daniel 2:1-13 sets the stage. King Nebuchadnezzar has dreams one night that leave him troubled and unable to sleep even though he cannot remember them. He summons all the magicians, conjurers, and sorcerers in his court and commands them to tell him what he dreamed and also to give him the interpretation. When the king's wise men protest that no one could tell the king his dream, Nebuchadnezzar becomes enraged and immediately orders the execution of all the wise men in the land, including Daniel and his three friends, Shadrach, Meshach, and Abednego. Observe the process Daniel goes through to fulfill the king's command (and save many lives in the process!).

First, *Daniel determined the source of the dreams.*

Then Daniel replied with discretion and discernment to Arioch, the captain of the king's bodyguard, who had gone forth to slay the wise men of Babylon; he said to Arioch, the king's commander, "For what reason is the decree from the king so urgent?" Then Arioch informed Daniel about the matter.[174]

Daniel determined that this was his assignment in God and that there was a revelatory message from God in the king's dreams that he was to find. This is always the first critical step. Determine the source!

Having determined the source of the dream, *Daniel asked for time to interpret it.*

So Daniel went in and requested of the king that he would give him time, in order that he might declare the interpretation to the king.

We are the recipients of divine wisdom. No one has it except Spirit-filled believers in Jesus! Seek the Lord, and seek His godly counselors. As the apostle Paul wrote, "Yet we do speak wisdom among those who are mature; a wisdom, however, not of this age nor of the rulers of this age, who are passing away."

After the king granted Daniel the "grace period" that he requested, *Daniel rallied people to pray.*

Then Daniel went to his house and informed his friends, Hananiah, Mishael and Azariah, about the matter, so that they might request compassion from the God of heaven concerning this mystery, so that Daniel and his friends would not be destroyed with the rest of the wise men of Babylon. [177]

They "request[ed] compassion" from God; what an awesome phrase! They asked God to reveal the "mystery." Intercession always pays off!

With intercessors in place and in action, *Daniel received revelation from the Lord.*

Then the mystery was revealed to Daniel in a night vision. [178]

The simplicity of that statement is mind-boggling! It is so matter of fact, as if receiving revelation in a night vision is the most natural thing in the world! But it is *supernatural.* Only God can do such a thing! Mysteries invite intrigue, but only God can release the meaning.

When he realized that their prayers had been answered, *Daniel worshiped his God.*

Then Daniel blessed the God of heaven; Daniel said, "Let the name of God be blessed forever and ever, for wisdom and power belong to Him. It is He who changes the times and the epochs; He removes kings and establishes kings; He gives wisdom to wise men and knowledge to men of understanding. It is He who reveals the profound and hidden things; He knows what is in the darkness, and the light dwells with Him. To You, O God of my fathers, I give thanks and praise, for You have given me wisdom and power; even now You have made known to me what we requested of You, for You have made known to us the king's matter." [179]

Do you see the pattern? Daniel and his friends pray; God responds; they worship. This was a major key in Daniel's life; he was a *worshiper*. No wonder the Holy Spirit liked hanging out with Daniel! He worshiped the Lord as his source of revelation and wisdom. Daniel was a worshiper *before* the interpretation came. I think this is one of the reasons why God doused him with revelation, why God gave him the interpretation, and why God continued to entrust a stewardship to him as his sphere of influence kept growing and expanding.

After worshiping the Lord, Daniel announced that he was ready. Arioch ushered him into the king's presence, where *Daniel declared the mystery.*

Daniel answered before the king and said, "As for the mystery about which the king has inquired, neither wise men, conjurers, magicians nor diviners are able to declare it to the king. However, there is a God in heaven who reveals mysteries, and He has made known to King Nebuchadnezzar what will take place in the latter days. This was your dream and the visions in your mind while on your bed. As for you, O king, while on your bed your thoughts turned to what would take place in the future; and He who reveals mysteries has made known to you what will take place. But as for me, this mystery has not been revealed to me for any wisdom residing in me more than in any other living man, but for the purpose of making the interpretation known to the king, and that you may understand the thoughts of your mind."[180]

That was Daniel's declaration—a declaration of honor toward God and toward the king and of humility toward himself.

Daniel went on to describe the king's dream in detail: a huge statue with a head of gold, chest and arms of silver, abdomen and thighs of bronze, legs of iron, and feet of iron and clay mixed together. Then a stone *"cut out without hands"* crushed the statue to dust and then grew until it filled the entire earth.[181]

After describing the king's dream, *Daniel wisely interpreted the dream.*

"This was the dream; now we will tell its interpretation before the king. You, O king, are the king of kings, to whom the God of heaven has given the kingdom, the power, the strength and the glory; and wherever the sons of men dwell, or the beasts of the field, or the birds of

the sky, He has given them into your hand and has caused you to rule over them all. You are the head of gold."[182]

Daniel then proceeds to describe three other kingdoms, represented by the other parts of the statue, that will arise in succession after Babylon: the Medo-Persian Empire, the empire of Greece, and the Roman Empire. Finally, a fifth kingdom, represented by the stone "cut out without hands," will be established—an eternal Kingdom set up by God that eventually would crush and supplant all the kingdoms of men.[183] Daniel concludes his interpretation by giving glory to God:

"...the great God has made known to the king what will take place in the future; so the dream is true and its interpretation is trustworthy."[184]

Don't you just love the way that Daniel talks about God? Like Daniel, when we are interpreting a dream for someone else, we need to be sensitive in our approach as to how to interpret and deliver the message we have received. And we must always be careful to give God the glory.

Having successfully interpreted the king's dream, *Daniel received his reward.*

Then King Nebuchadnezzar fell on his face and did homage to Daniel, and gave orders to present to him an offering and fragrant incense. The king answered Daniel and said, "Surely your God is a God of gods and a Lord of kings and a revealer of mysteries, since you have been able to reveal this mystery." Then the king promoted Daniel and gave him many great gifts, and he made him ruler over the whole province of Babylon and chief prefect over all the wise men of Babylon. And Daniel made request of the king, and he appointed Shadrach, Meshach and Abed-nego over the administration of the province of Babylon, while Daniel was at the king's court.[185]

Daniel's example illustrates how we should handle our "trophies." When people try to exalt us for a word of wisdom or a word of knowledge or other revelation that was helpful to them, we should do as Daniel did and return them to the Lord. Daniel humbled himself and exalted God, and God elevated him.

A Voice That Can Be Heard

At times there is a struggle and a tension that we have to deal with in order to properly handle even the correct interpretation of dreams and revelation. Suppose more than one person receives a similar message or even the exact same content. Both individuals then present their truths to those intended. Why is one person received and recognized and another is not? Why is it that one person appears to be valued and others are not? What constitutes a "voice that can be heard"?

I have struggled with this personally. Years ago I would get revelation and present it to the intended person and get no reaction whatsoever from them. Somebody else would come along who had received something similar for the same person, and the next thing you know everyone was talking about what a powerful word he/she had received. What about the word I had received? Wasn't it just as powerful and just as valid?

This is a risk faced by everyone who aspires to walk in the realm of revelation and dream language. As a safeguard, we need to keep Daniel's example before us constantly: his complete absence of ego and self-ambition because he knew that it was all about God and not about him.

I want to share with you some helpful hints for cultivating a "voice that can be heard" that I have learned by trial and error and out of my own stress, turmoil, heartache, and pain. In other words, these are lessons from the woodshed!

1. It is the strategic purpose and timing of God for one and not necessarily the other to be promoted. This deals with promotion. We each have different times and seasons in our lives.

2. For one it is a season of favor while for the other it is a season of testing—of character formation and preparation. This is often the time when God seems silent. But remember, the teacher is always silent when you are taking a test.

3. There is a strategic joining relationally that is to occur with the dreamer and/or interpreter and the recipient of the revelation. The reason one person's voice is heard and acted on while yours is not may be because God has in His purpose a relationship that is supposed to unfold between that other person and the recipient, a relationship with ramifications far beyond the dream and its interpretation.

4. One has a sphere that includes a higher public profile while another's sphere is the intercessor's closet. Both are vitally

important to God's purpose, but we are dealing with the wisdom ways of God, and the way He deals with one may be different from the way He deals with another.

5. For one it is divine protection while for the other it is graduation. God will not promote you before you are ready. If He does not promote you, it is for your own protection. He will not catapult you into the public arena with its stress and pressure and spiritual warfare issues that you cannot yet handle. Be patient; when the time comes, God will graduate you.

6. For one there has been an accumulation of investment. That person has a history and a track record. The other is just getting started. There is no track record yet, no reputation yet for integrity and reliability, no gauge yet for judging trustworthiness.

7. For one there is a relational bridge of trust while the other's bridge has been damaged or remains untested.

8. While the content might be the same, the manner of delivery is not. The leader/recipient always has the choice of which style he/she wishes to have promoted publicly in his/her house, church, or sphere of authority. Just because your voice is not being heard in one place or venue does not mean it will not be heard in another.

9. Some things remain a mystery! We are never exempt from trusting in the Lord with all our heart and not leaning on our own understanding. It is His business. Let God be God! Learn to thank Him that you have been used as a voice of confirmation. Let Him be your affirmation!

Presenting a Dream to a King

Want to give a word to a king? Want to be used to interpret a king's dream? Want to be brought before people of influence? How would you carry a message to such a person? With these questions in mind, consider the follow thoughts.

You must have the character to carry the gift. The issues of integrity and honor are of utmost importance when approaching a king or other person of influence! Humility, internal security, and trust in God are essential. When studying the life of Daniel, Joseph, Esther, and others, you will find that the way of approach can be as important as the message that is brought. Being a "voice that can be heard" deals as much with "prophetic protocol" as it does with content. Yet, walking in the fear of the Lord versus the fear of man is also critical.

Every believer in Christ Jesus is a priest and a king. *"To Him who loves us and released us from our sins by His blood—and He has made us to be a kingdom, priests to His God and Father—to Him be the glory and the dominion forever and ever. Amen."*[186] Since this is the case, whenever you approach any of God's children—no matter who or where they are—treat them with dignity, integrity, honor, and humility. Remember, they are kings or queens in God's eyes...and so are you!

God is our ultimate King! Want to give God a word? How does a priestly watchman give his Commander-in-chief a word? Yes, use the same heart qualities of honor and humility mixed with boldness as you approach the gracious courts of the King. Prophetic intercession is the means of giving the King of the universe a word of consultation or an appeal for intervention and direction. Join others and me in the amazing art of intervention by presenting your dreams before the King of Kings!

Things to Do Always With Dreams

In closing, let me leave you with some final counsel in the wisdom ways of handling dreams and dream language.

Earnestly desire the gifts of the Holy Spirit. Paul wrote, *"Pursue love, yet desire earnestly spiritual gifts, but especially that you may prophesy."*[187] The phrase *"desire earnestly"* means to pursue passionately, to have a deep-seated craving for. Have a deep-seated craving to prophesy (which includes dreams). Not only does God want to speak *to* you, He also wants to speak *through* you! Be a dreamer for God's sake! Volunteer!

Believe God's prophets and you will succeed. *"Jehoshaphat stood and said, 'Listen to me, O Judah and inhabitants of Jerusalem, put your trust in the Lord your God and you will be established. Put your trust in His prophets and succeed."*[188] This verse, Second Chronicles 20:20, gives us "20/20" vision. Rejoice! What a privilege you have been given. Mix faith with God's Word and receive the Lord's results. But place your faith in the "God of the Word," not the "man of the word."

Pray the promise back to God. Follow Daniel's example of reminding God of His Word through intercession.[189] Bathe your dream experience in prayer.[190]

Fight the good fight. Use the Word revealed through a dream as equipment for spiritual battle. *"This command I entrust to you, Timothy, my son, in accordance with the prophecies previously made concerning you, that by them you fight the good fight."*[191] Do spiritual warfare against discouragement, doubt, unbelief, and fear through declaring and reciting what the prophetic dream states concerning you.

Seek confirmation at all times. Remember, out of the mouth of two or three witnesses every fact is to be confirmed and established. The Bible states in *three* places that God confirms His Word by *three* witnesses![192]

And finally, *dare to believe and then obey!* Are you a believing believer? Are you listening and then obeying? "Obedience is the expression of faith and the key to learning to recognize God's voice ever more clearly. We need to be willing to risk those little mistakes as we venture in faith, and trust God to protect us from the big ones."[193]

Come on a great adventure with Michal Ann and me on *understanding dream language!* Receive the spirit of revelation and be a dreamer! Step out on the limb of faith, and let's do something for Jesus' sake! God is the one who promised to pour out His Spirit on all flesh in the Last Days. It is His will to give dreams and visions and revelations![194]

After all, dreams are our Last-Days inheritance!

Behold, here comes another dreamer!

Reflection Questions

1. How are we to wisely respond to dreams and revelation? What are some of the practical tips listed?

2. What are some of the keys we should keep in mind when presenting a dream to a king?

3. In closing, what are some things that you should *always* do with dreams?

Referral Reading

Jane Hamon, *Dreams and Vision* (Ventura, CA: Regal Books, 2000).

Doug Addison, *Prophecy, Dreams, and Evangelism* (North Sutton, NH: Streams Publishing House, 2005).

Jim W. Goll, *The Coming Prophetic Revolution* (Grand Rapids, MI: Chosen Books, 2003).

ABOUT THE AUTHORS

James (Jim) W. Goll is the cofounder of Encounters Network (formerly Ministry to the Nations) with his wife Michal Ann. They are members of the Harvest International Ministries Apostolic Team and contributing writers for *Kairos Magazine* and other periodicals. James and Michal Ann have four wonderful children and live in the beautiful rolling hills of Franklin, Tennessee.

James has produced several study guides on subjects such as Equipping in the Prophetic, Blueprints for Prayer, and Empowered for Ministry, which are all available through the Encounters Resource Center.

Other books by Jim W. and Michal Ann Goll include:

Fire on the Altar

The Lost Art of Intercession

Kneeling on the Promises

Wasted on Jesus

Exodus Cry

Elijah's Revolution

The Coming Prophetic Revolution

Women on the Frontlines—A Call to Courage

A Call to the Secret Place

Intercession

The Beginner's Guide to Hearing God

The Seer

God Encounters

Praying for Israel's Destiny

For more information, contact:

ENCOUNTERS NETWORK

P.O. Box 1653

Franklin, TN 37075

Office Phone: 615-599-5552

Office Fax: 615-599-5554

For orders call: 1-877-200-1604

For more information or to sign up for monthly e-mail communiques, please visit www.encountersnetwork.com or send an e-mail to: info@encountersnetwork.com.

ENDNOTES

1. Psalm 19:1, emphasis added.

2. Psalm 8:3-4, emphasis added.

3. Psalm 139:13-14, emphasis added.

4. Mark 4:10-12.

5. Mark 4:22-25.

6. Numbers 12:6.

7. Job 33:14-16.

8. Joel 2:28-29.

9. Jim W. Goll, *The Seer: The Prophetic Power of Visions, Dreams, and Open Heavens* (Shippensburg, PA: Destiny Image Publishers, Inc., 2004), 57-58.

10. Goll, *The Seer*, 59.

11. Acts 2:17.

12. Goll, The Seer, 60.

13. 1 Timothy 2:4.

14. Genesis 15:12-17.

15. Genesis 28:10-22.

16. 1 Kings 3:5-15.

17. Acts 16:9-15.

18. Jeremiah 23:16, emphasis added.

19. Proverbs 25:2.

20. James 1:21, emphasis added.

21. John 5:19-20.

22. Romans 6:13-16.

23. Ephesians 1:17-19.

24. 2 Kings 6:17.

25. Genesis 40:8.

26. For a fuller account of Michal Ann's experience, refer to our book *God Encounters* (Shippensburg, PA: Destiny Image Publishers, Inc., 2005) and Michal Ann's book *Women on the Frontlines* (Shippensburg, PA: Destiny Image Publishers, Inc., 1998).

27. Hebrews 13:8.

28. James 1:17.

29. Morton T. Kelsey, *God, Dreams, and Revelation: A Christian Interpretation of Dreams* (Minneapolis, MN: Augsburg, 1991), 32-33.

30. Kelsey, *God, Dreams, and Revelation*, 32.

31. Kelsey, *God, Dreams, and Revelation*, 33.

32. Kelsey, *God, Dreams, and Revelation*, 35.

33. Kelsey, *God, Dreams, and Revelation*, 43.

34. Deuteronomy 18:18.

35. Deuteronomy 18:22.

36. 1 John 4:1.

37. The basic content in this section is adapted from Vanessa L. Ochs with Elizabeth Ochs, *The Jewish Dream Book: The Key to Opening the Inner Meaning of Your Dreams* (Woodstock, VT: Jewish Lights Publishing, 2003), 35-46.

38. Ochs, *The Jewish Dream Book*, 35.

39. Ochs, *The Jewish Dream Book*, 35.

40. Ochs, *The Jewish Dream Book*, 36.

41. Ochs, *The Jewish Dream Book*, 39.

42. Ochs, *The Jewish Dream Book*, 39.

43. Ochs, *The Jewish Dream Book*, 39-40.

44. Ochs, *The Jewish Dream Book*, 40.

45. Ochs, *The Jewish Dream Book*, 44.

46. Ochs, *The Jewish Dream Book*, 44-45.

47. Ochs, *The Jewish Dream Book*, 45.

48. Ochs, *The Jewish Dream Book*, 46.

49. Luke 18:17, NKJV.

50. Matthew 1:18-25; 2:13, 19-23.

51. Matthew 2:12.

52. Acts 9:1-9.

53. Acts 9:10-18.

54. Acts 16:9-10.

55. Acts 10:1-45.

56. Kelsey, *God, Dreams, and Revelation*, 101.

57. Kelsey, *God, Dreams, and Revelation*, 104.

58. Kelsey, *God, Dreams, and Revelation*, 104-105.

59. Louis M. Savary, Patricia H. Berne, and Strephon Kaplan Williams, *Dreams and Spiritual Growth: A Judeo-Christian Way of Dreamwork* (Mahwah, NJ: Paulist Press, 1984), 39.

60. Clement of Alexandria, quoted in Kelsey, *God, Dreams, and Revelation*, 106.

61. Savary, *Dreams and Spiritual Growth*, 39.

62. Savary, *Dreams and Spiritual Growth*, 41.

63. Kelsey, *God, Dreams, and Revelation*, 134.

64. Kelsey, *God, Dreams, and Revelation*, 134.

65. Savary, *Dreams and Spiritual Growth*, 54.

66. Savary, *Dreams and Spiritual Growth*, 55-56.

67. Thomas Aquinas, quoted in *Savary, Dreams and Spiritual Growth*, 56.

68. Kelsey, *God, Dreams, and Revelation*, 161-162.

69. A.J. Gordon, *How Christ Came to Church: A Spiritual Autobiography* (New York, NY: Revell, 1895), 63, quoted in Kelsey, *God, Dreams, and Revelation*, 163-164.

70. John 10:10.

71. 1 John 3:8.

72. Matthew 24:43.

73. John 10:1.

74. James 4:7.

75. Kelsey, *God, Dreams, and Revelation*, 191-192.

76. Ecclesiastes 4:6.

77. Isaiah 30:15.

78. Ephesians 4:23-25.

79. Psalm 37:8.

80. Ephesians 4:26-27.

81. Romans 13:10,13-14.

82. Ephesians 5:18.

83. Hebrews 12:15.

84. Ephesians 4:30.

85. Mark 4:24b.

86. Philippians 4:8.

87. Matthew 13:12.

88. Matthew 13:16.

89. Information in this section is adapted from Chuck D. Pierce and Rebecca Wagner Sytsema, *When God Speaks: How to Interpret Dreams, Visions, Signs and Wonders* (Ventura, CA: Regal Books, 2005), 63-65.

90. Colossians 3:2.

91. See Song of Solomon 2:15.

92. Hosea 4:6.

93. Mark 9:24.

94. Pierce, *When God Speaks,* 64-65.

95. Mark Rutland, *Dream: Awake or Asleep, Unlock the Power of God's Vision* (Lake Mary, FL: Charisma House, 2003), 8-9.

96. Hebrews 9:11-12.

97. Jude 20.

98. Joshua 1:8.

99. John 4:23.

100. 2 Chronicles 20:18-22.

101. John 16:13.

102. 1 Corinthians 12:4-7.

103. 2 Corinthians 10:13.

104. Romans 12:3.

105. Proverbs 18:16.

106. Jeremiah 17:9.

107. Matthew 12:34b, NKJV.

108. See Genesis 20:1-18.

109. 1 Timothy 4:1.

110. Pierce, *When God Speaks*, 80-81.

111. John 14:16-17.

112. John 14:26.

113. John 15:26.

114. John 16:7.

115. John 16:13-15.

116. Jim W. Goll, *The Beginner's Guide to Hearing God* (Ventura, CA, Regal Books, 2004), 24-25.

117. James 4:2b.

118. James 1:5.

119. Matthew 7:8.

120. Colossians 1:11, AMP.

121. 1 Samuel 28:1-25.

122. Joy Parrott, *Parables in the Night Seasons: Understanding Your Dreams* (Renton, WA: Glory Publications, Joy Parrott Ministries, 2002), 57-58.

123. Dr. Joe Ibojie, *Dreams and Visions: How to Receive, Interpret, and Apply Your Dreams* (San Giovanni Teatino (Ch), Italy: Destiny Image Europe, 2005), 160.

124. Parrott, *Parables in the Night Seasons*, 58-59.

125. Jeremiah 33:3.

126. Rutland, *Dream: Awake or Asleep*, 59.

127. Genesis 40:8.

128. Daniel 1:17,20.

129. Daniel 5:1-31.

130. 1 Chronicles 12:32.

131. Revelation 13:18, NKJV.

132. John 19:30.

133. Matthew 13:31-32.

134. Revelation 5:8; 8:3-4.

135. Luke 8:11.

136. Revelation 1:20.

137. For more information on this subject, see Goll, *The Seer*.

138. 1 Corinthians 2:14, NKJV.

139. Psalm 63:6.

140. Psalm 77:12.

141. Psalm 119:15.

142. Psalm 143:5.

143. William Burroughs.

144. Rutland, *Dream: Awake or Asleep*, 8.

145. Charles William Dement.

146. Rutland, *Dream: Awake or Asleep*, 38.

147. Ecclesiastes 5:7.

148. Herman Riffel, *Learning to Hear God's Voice* (Old Tappan, NJ: Chosen Books, 1986), 144-145.

149. Riffel, *Learning to Hear God's Voice*, 147-148.

150. Revelation 1:10.

151. Habakkuk 2:1-3.

152. Daniel 7:1.

153. Job 20:8.

154. Psalm 46:10a, KJV.

155. 1 Peter 5:7.

156. Habakkuk 1:1.

157. Matthew 15:21-24.

158. Matthew 27:46b.

159. John 5:1-9.

160. Matthew 15:25-28.

161. Proverbs 12:8a.

162. Revelation 8:13; 14:6; 19:17.

163. 2 Corinthians 12:2.

164. See also Galatians 6:1 and Second Timothy 2:23-26.

165. Proverbs 9:10.

166. See Revelation 12:10 and Proverbs 10:18.

167. 1 Peter 5:8.

168. Bart Druckenmiller, *Dreams in the Spirit: Seeing Your World Through Heaven's Eyes*, Volume Two (Shippensburg, PA: Treasure House, an imprint of Destiny Image Publishers, Inc., 2002), 220.

169. For a more in-depth discussion of responding to dreams, refer to: Jim W. Goll, *The Coming Prophetic Revolution: A Call for Passionate, Consecrated Warriors* (Old Tappan, NJ: Chosen Books, 2001).

170. This list is adapted from Ibojie, *Dreams and Visions*, 89-91.

171. Ibojie, *Dreams and Visions*, 90.

172. Daniel 12:4.

173. The outline for the discussion of Daniel in this section is adapted from Pierce, *When God Speaks*, 81-83.

174. Daniel 2:14-15.

175. Daniel 2:16.

176. 1 Corinthians 2:6.

177. Daniel 2:17-18.

178. Daniel 2:19a.

179. Daniel 2:19b-23.

180. Daniel 2:27-30.

181. Daniel 2:31-35.

182. Daniel 2:36-38.

183. Daniel 2:39-44.

184. Daniel 2:45b.

185. Daniel 2:46-49.

186. Revelation 1:5b-6.

187. 1 Corinthians 14:1.

188. 2 Chronicles 20:20.

189. See Jeremiah 29:10; Daniel 9:1-19.

190. For deeper study on this topic, see Jim W. Goll, *Kneeling on the Promises: Birthing God's Purposes Through Prophetic Intercession* (Old Tappan, NJ: Chosen Books, 1999).

191. 1 Timothy 1:18.

192. See Deuteronomy 19:15; Matthew 18:16; 2 Corinthians 13:1.

193. Riffel, *Learning to Hear God's Voice*, 143.

194. See Joel 2:28; Acts 2:17-18.

DREAM SYMBOLS AND THEIR INTERPRETATIONS

The following material is not intended to be an official dictionary of definitions, but rather a tool to be flexibly used in the hands of believers under the leadership of the Holy Spirit. Thanks goes to numerous pioneers who have a blazed a trail in understanding these ways of God. People such as Kevin Connor, Herman Riffel, John Paul Jackson, Ira Milligan, Jane Hamon, Chuck Pierce and others have indeed been forerunners for us all. Over time, you will grow in your interpretive grace and you will add some of your own understandings to the following dream symbols and their interpretations.

ACID - Bitter, offense, carrying a grudge, hatred, sarcasm.

ALLIGATOR - Ancient, evil out of the past (through inherited or personal sin), danger, destruction, evil spirit.

ALTAR - A symbol for sacrifice and for incense.

ANCHOR - Representaion of safety and hope.

ARM - Represents God's power and strength.

ARMOR - A symbol of warfare.

ASHES - Memories, repentance, ruin, destruction.

AUTOMOBILE - Life, person, ministry.

AUTUMN - End, completion, change, repentance.

AXE - Represents warfare and judgment.

BABY - New beginning, new idea, dependent, helpless, innocent, sin.

BALANCE(S) - Represents judgment.

BARN - Symbol for blessings.

BAT - Witchcraft, unstable, flighty, fear.

BEARD - Represents old age and wisdom.

BEAVER - Industrious, busy, diligent, clever, ingenious.

BED - Rest, salvation, meditation, intimacy, peace, covenant (marriage, natural or evil), self-made.

BICYCLE - Works, works of the flesh, legalism, self-righteousness, working out life's difficulties, messenger.

BIRD - Symbol of spirits, good or evil, see the parable of Jesus on the birds.

BLACK - Symbol of famine and death.

BLOOD - Symbol for sacrifice and for life (life is in the blood).

BLUE - Symbol of Heaven.

BOW - Usually represents judgment.

BREAD - Represents life.

BRICK - Represents slavery and human effort.

BRIDLE - Symbol of restraint, control.

BROTHER-IN-LAW - Partiality or adversary, fellow minister, problem relationship, partner, oneself, natural brother-in-law.

BROWN - Dead (as in plant life), repentant, born again, without spirit.

BULL - Persecution, spiritual warfare, opposition, accusation, slander, threat, economic increase.

BUTTERFLY - Freedom, flighty, fragile, temporary glory.

CAMEL - Represents servanthood, bearing the burden of others.

CANDLE - Symbol of light (Holy Spirit or the spirit of man).

CANDLESTICK - Represents the Church.

CAT - Self-willed, untrainable, predator, unclean spirit, bewitching charm, stealthy, sneaky, deception, self-pity, something precious in the context of a personal pet.

CATERPILLAR - Represents judgment and destructive powers.

CENSER - Symbol of intercession and worship.

CHAIN - Symbol of binding, oppression, punishment.

CHICKEN - Fear, cowardliness; hen can be protection, gossip, motherhood; rooster can be boasting, bragging, proud; chick can be defenseless, innocent.

CIRCLE - Symbol of eternity.

CITY - Symbol of security, safety, permanency, (cities of refuge).

CLOUD and FIERY PILLAR - Represents Divine presence, covering and guidance.

COLT - Represents bearing burden of others or could be a portrayal of stubbornness.

CORN (Oil and Wine) - Represents blessings of God.

CROW (raven) - Confusion, outspoken, operating in envy or strife, hateful, direct path, unclean, God's minister of justice or provision.

CUP - Symbol of life, health, or could represent death and evil .

CYMBAL - Symbol of vibration, praise, worship.

DEER - Graceful, swift, sure-footed, agile, timid.

DESERT - Desolation, temptation, solitude.

DOG - Unbelievers, religious hypocrites.

DOOR - An opening, entrance.

DOVE - Holy Spirit.

DRAGON - Satan.

DREAMING - A message within a message, aspiration, vision.

DROWNING - Overcome, self-pity, depression, grief, sorrow, temptation, excessive debt.

DRUGS - Influence, spell, sorcery, witchcraft, control, legalism, medicine, healing.

EIGHT - New beginnings.

EIGHT-EIGHT-EIGHT - The first resurrection saints.

ELEPHANT - Invincible or thick-skinned, not easily offended, powerful, large.

ELEVATOR - Changing position, going into the spirit realm, elevated, demoted.

ELEVEN - Incompleteness, disorder.

EYE(S) - Omniscience, knowledge, sight, insight, foresight.

FACE - Character, countenance.

FALLING - Unsupported, loss of support (financial, moral, public), trial, succumb, backsliding.

FATHER - Authority, God, author, originator, source, inheritance, tradition, custom, Satan, natural father.

FATHER-IN-LAW - Law, authoritative relationship based on law, legalism, problem authoritative relationship, natural father-in-law.

FEATHERS - Covering, protection.

FEET - Heart, walk, way, thoughts (meditation), offense, stubborn (unmovable), rebellion (kicking), sin.

FIFTY - Symbol of liberty, freedom, Pentecost.

FIG - Relates to Israel as a nation.

FIG LEAVES - Self-atonement, self-made covering.

FINGER - Feeling, sensitivity, discernment, conviction, works, accusation (as in pointing a finger), instruction.

FIRE - Presence of God, Holiness of God, purifying, testing.

FIVE - God's grace to man, responsibility of man.

FISH - Souls of men.

FLIES - Evil spirits, filth of satan's kingdom. Beelzebub – "Lord of flies."

FLOOD - Judgment on sin and violence (The flood from Noah's time).

FLOWER - Fading glory of man.

FOREST - Symbol of nations.

FORTRESS - Protection, a stronghold.

FORTY - Symbol of testing, trial, closing in victory or defeat (Israel in Wilderness and Jesus on the desert).

FORTY-TWO - Israel's oppression, the Lord's advent to the earth.

FORTY-FIVE - Preservation.

FOUNTAIN - Source of life, refreshing.

FOUR - Represents worldwide, universal (as in 4 corners of the earth).

FOURTEEN - Passover, time of testing.

FOX - Cunning, evil men.

FRIEND - Self, the character or circumstance of one's friend reveals something about oneself; sometimes one friend represents another (look for the same name, initials, hair color); sometimes represents actual friend.

FROG - Demons, unclean spirits.

GARDEN - Growth and fertility.

GATE - A way of entrance, power, authority.

GOLD - Kingship, kingdom glory, God or gods.

GRANDCHILD - Heir, oneself, inherited blessing or iniquity, one's spiritual legacy, actual grandchild.

GRANDPARENT - Past, spiritual inheritance (good or evil), actual grandparent.

GRAPES - Fruit of the vine, cup of the Lord.

GRASS - Frailty of the flesh.

GRASSHOPPER - Destruction.

GREEN - Prosperity, growth, life.

HAMMER - Word of God.

HAND - Symbol of strength, power, action, possession.

HARP - Praise, worship to God.

HEAD - Authority, thoughts, mind.

HEART - Emotions, motivations, desires.

HELMET - Protection for thoughts, mind.

HEN - One who gathers, protects.

HILLS - Elevation, high, loftiness.

HORN - Power, strength, defense.

HORSE - Power, strength, conquest.

HOUSE - Home, dwelling place, the Church.

INCENSE - Prayer, intercessions and worship.

JEWELS - People of God.

KEY - Authority, power to bind or loose, lock or unlock.

KISS - Agreement, covenant, enticement, betrayal, covenant breaker, deception, seduction, friend.

KNEE - Reverence, humility.

LADDER - Christ connecting Heaven and earth.

LAMB - Humility, the Church, Christ.

LEAD - Weight, wickedness, sin, burden, judgment, fool, foolishness.

LEAF - Life amidst propserity.

LEGS - Man's walk, man's strength.

LEOPARD - Swiftness, usually associated with vengeance.

LILIES - Beauty, majesty.

LION - Royalty and Kingship bravery, confidence.

LIPS - Witness.

MECHANIC - Minister, Christ, prophet, pastor, counselor.

MICE - Devourer, curse, plague, timid.

MILK - Foundational truth, nourishment.

MIRROR - God's Word or one's heart, looking at oneself, looking back, memory, past, vanity.

MISCARRIAGE - Abort, failure, loss, repentance, unjust judgment.

MONEY - Power, provision, wealth, natural talents and skills, spiritual riches, power, authority, trust in human strength, covetousness.

MONKEY - Foolishness, clinging, mischief, dishonesty, addiction.

MOON - Symbol of light in darkness, sign of the Son of Man.

MOTH - Symbol of destruction.

MOTHER - Source, Church, love, kindness, spiritual or natural mother.

MOTHER-IN-LAW - Legalism, meddler, trouble, natural mother-in-law.

MOUNTAIN - Kingdoms, dignity, permanence.

MOUTH - Witness, good or evil.

NAIL - Security, establish.

NECK - Force, loveliness, or inflexibility, meekness, rebellion.

NEST - Home, place to dwell.

NET - Symbol of a catcher as in the parables, catching men.

NINE - Judgment, finality.

NINETEEN - Barren, ashamed, repentant, selflessness, without self-righteousness; faith.

NOSE - Breath, discernment.

NUDITY - Uncovered or flesh, self-justification, self-righteousness, impure, ashamed, stubborn, temptation, lust, sexual control, exhibitionism, truth, honest, nature.

OIL - Holy Spirit, anointing.

ONE - God as a unity and as a source, new beginnings.

ONE HUNDRED - Fullness, full measure, full recompense, full reward; God's election of grace, children of promise.

ONE HUNDRED NINETEEN - The resurrection day; Lord's day.

ONE HUNDRED TWENTY - End of all flesh, beginning of life in the Spirit; divine period of probation.

ONE HUNDRED FORTY-FOUR - God's ultimate in creation.

ONE HUNDRED - Revival, ingathering, final harvest of souls.

ORANGE - Danger, great jeopardy, harm; a common color combination is orange and black, which usually signifies great evil or danger; bright or fire orange can be power, force, energy.

ONE THOUSAND - Maturity, full stature, mature service, mature judgment; divine completeness and the glory of God.

OVEN - Testing, or judgment.

PALACE - Heaven, royalty.

PALM TREE - Victory, worship.

PASTURE - Places of spiritual nourishment.

PEARL - Spiritual truth.

PEN/PENCIL - Tongue, indelible words, covenant, agreement, contract, vow, publish, record, permanent, unforgettable, gossip.

PIG - Ignorance, hypocrisy, religious unbelievers, unclean people, selfish, gluttonous, vicious, vengeful.

PILLAR - Strength, steadfastness, assistance.

PINK - Flesh, sensual, immoral, moral (as in a heart of flesh); chaste, a female infant.

PIT - Prison, oppression.

PLUMBLINE - Standards of God, measuring of a life.

PLOW - Breaking new ground.

PREGNANCY - In process, sin or righteousness in process, desire, anticipation, expectancy.

PUMPKIN - Witchcraft, deception, snare, witch, trick.

PURPLE - Royalty, wealth, prosperity.

RABBIT - Increase, fast growth, multiplication; hare can be satan and his evil spirits.

RACCOON - Mischief, night raider, rascal, thief, bandit, deceitful.

RAIN - Blessing, God's Word and revival.

RAINBOW - Covenant.

RAM - Sacrifice.

RAVEN - Evil, satan.

RED - Suffering, sacrifice or sin.

RINGS - Eternity, completion.

RIVER - Revival, refreshing.

ROACH - Infestation, unclean spirits, hidden sin.

ROBE - Covering, royalty.

ROCK - Christ our rock, stability.

ROD - Rule, correction, guidance.

ROOF - Covering, oversight.

ROOT - Spiritual source, offspring.

ROPE - Binding, bondage.

ROSE - Christ and His Church.

RUBIES - Value, worth, significance.

SALT - Incorruptibility, preserve from corruption, covenant.

SAND - Similar to seed, generations.

SAPPHIRE - Beauty, value.

SCORPION - Evil spirits, evil men; pinch of pain.

SEA - Wicked nations.

SERPENT - Satan and evil spirits.

SEVEN - Completeness, perfection.

SEVENTEEN - Spiritual order, incomplete, immature, undeveloped, childish, victory.

SEVENTY - Number of increase, perfected ministry.

SHEEP - Chant, the people of God, innocent.

SHIELD - Sign of protection.

SHOE - Sign of walking, protection for your walk.

SHOULDER - Bearing the burden of another, authority, rulership.

SISTER - Spiritual sister, Church, self, natural sister.

SIX-SIX-SIX - Sign of the Mark of the Beast, Antichrist.

SIXTEEN - Free-spirited, without boundaries, without law, without sin, salvation; love.

SIXTY - Pride.

SIXTY-SIX - Idol worship.

SIX HUNDRED - Warfare.

SKINS - Covering.

SMOKE - Blinding power.

SNOW - Spotlessness, radiance.

SPARROW - Small value but precious.

SPRING - New beginning, revival, fresh start, renewal, regeneration, salvation, refreshing.

STARS - Israel, generations.

STEPS - Signs of spiritual progress.

STONE - Might, permanence.

STORMS - Misfortune, difficulty, trials.

SUMMER - Harvest, opportunity, trial, heat of affliction.

SUN - Glory, brightness, light, Christ.

SWORD - Scriptures, Christ.

TEETH - Consuming power.

TEN - Law and order.

TENT - A temporary covering, not a permanent home.

TIGER - Danger, powerful minister (both good and evil).

TIN - Dross, waste, worthless, cheap, purification.

THIRTEEN - Sign of rebellion, backsliding, apostasy .

THIRTY - Maturity for ministry.

THIRTY-TWO - Covenant.

THIRTY-THREE - Promise.

THIRTY-FOUR - Naming of a son.

THIRTY-FIVE - Hope.

THIRTY-SIX - Enemy.

THIRTY-SEVEN - The Word of God.

THIRTY-EIGHT - Slavery.

THIRTY-NINE - Disease.

THREE-HUNDRED - Faithful remnant (Gideon's army).

TONGUE - Language, speeech.

TRAIN - Continuous, unceasing work, connected, fast, Church.

TRAP - Snare, danger, trick.

TREES - Nations, individuals, the Church.

TUNNEL - Passage, transition, way of escape, troubling experience, trial, hope.

TWELVE - Divine government, apostolic government.

TWENTY-ONE - Exceeding sinfulness, of sin.

TWENTY-FOUR - Symbol of Priesthood courses and order.

TWENTY-TWO - Light.

TWENTY-THREE - Death.

TWENTY-FIVE - The forgiveness of sins.

TWENTY-SIX - The gospel of Christ.

TWENTY-SEVEN - Preaching of the Gospel.

TWENTY-EIGHT - Eternal life.

TWENTY-NINE - Departure.

TWO - Sign for witness, testimony, or unity.

TWO HUNDRED - Insufficiency.

VAN - Family (natural or Church), family ministry, fellowship.

VINE - Symbol for Israel, Christ and His Church.

VULTURE - Sign of uncleanness and devourer .

WALL - Fortification, division, refuge.

WATCH - Prophetic, intercession, being on guard.

WATERS - Nations of earth; agitation, under-currents, cross-currents.

WELL - Places of refreshment, source of water of life.

WHEEL - Transport, a circle, speed, spiritual activity.

WINTER - Barren, death, dormant, waiting, cold, unfriendly.

WHIRLWIND - Hurricane, sweeping power, unable to resist.

WIND - Breath of life, power of God.

WINDOW - Blessings of Heaven, openness.

WINE - Holy Spirit.

WINE-SKIN - Spiritual structure.

WINGS - Protection, spiritual transport.

WOLF - Satan and evil, false ministries, and teachers.

WOMAN - Church, virgin or harlot.

WOOD - Humanity.

WRESTLING - Striving, deliverance, resistance, persistence, trial, tribulation, spirit attempting to gain control.

YELLOW - Gift, marriage, family, honor, deceitful gift, timidity, fear, cowardliness.

YOKE - Servitude, slavery, or fellowship.

DIRECTIONS:

EAST - Beginning: Law (therefore blessed or cursed); birth; first Gen. 11:2; Job 38:24.

FRONT - Future or Now: (As in FRONT YARD) In the presence of; prophecy; immediate; current. Gen. 6:11; Rev. 1:19.

NORTH - Spiritual: Judgment; heaven; spiritual warfare (as in "taking your inheritance"). Prov. 25:23; Jer. 1:13-14.

LEFT - Spiritual: Weakness (of man), and therefore God's strength or ability; rejected. (Left Turn = spiritual change). Judg. 3:20-21; 2 Cor. 12:9,10.

SOUTH - Natural: Sin; world; temptation; trial; flesh; corruption; deception. Josh. 10:40; Job 37:9.

RIGHT - Natural: Authority; power; the strength of man (flesh) or the power of God revealed through man; accepted. (Right Turn = natural change). Matt. 5:29a, 30a; 1 Pet. 3:22.

WEST - End: Grace; death; last; conformed. Exod. 10:19; Luke 12:54.

BACK - Past: As in BACKYARD or BACKDOOR. Previous event or experience (good or evil); that which is behind (in time—for example, past sins or the sins of forefathers); unaware; unsuspecting; hidden; memory. Gen. 22:13; Josh. 8:4.

PEOPLE/RELATIVES/TRADES

BABY - New: Beginning; work; idea; the Church; sin; innocent; dependant; helpless; natural baby. 1 Cor. 3:1; Isa. 43:19.

CARPENTER - Builder: Preacher; evangelist; laborer (good or evil); Christ. 2 Kings 22:6; Isa. 41:7.

DOCTOR - Healer: Christ; preacher; authority; medical doctor, when naturally interpreted. Mark 2:17; 2 Chron. 16:12.

DRUNK - Influenced: Under a spell (i.e., under the influence of the Holy Spirit or a demon's spirit); controlled; fool; stubborn; rebellious; witchcraft. Eph. 5 :18; Prov. 14:16.

EMPLOYER - Servants: Pastor, Christ; satan; actual employer, when naturally interpreted. Col. 3:22; 2 Pet. 2:19.

GIANT - Strongman: Stronghold, challenge; obstacle; trouble. Num. 13:32-33.

INDIAN - First: Flesh (as in "the old man"); firstborn; chief; fierce; savvy; native. Col. 3:9; Gen. 49:3.

POLICE - Authority: Natural (civil) or spiritual authority (pastors, etc.), good or evil; protection; angels or demons; an enforcer of a curse of the Law. Rom. 13:1; Luke 12:11.

VEHICLES AND PARTS

AIRPLANE - Person or work: The Church; ministry; oversight (Soaring = Moved by the Spirit). Hab. 1:8; Judg. 13:25.

JET - Ministry or Minister: Powerful; fast. (Passenger jet = Church; Fighter = Individual person). Gen. 41:43; 2 Kings 10:16.

AUTOMOBILE - Life: Person; ministry (New car = New ministry or New way of life). Gen. 41:43; 2 Kings 10:16.

AUTO WRECK - Strife: Contention; conflict, calamity; mistake or sin in ministry (as in "failure to maintain right-of-way"). Nah. 2:4.

BICYCLE - Works: Works of the flesh (not of faith); self-righeousness; messenger. Gal. 5:4; Gal. 5:19.

BOAT - Church or personal ministry: (Sailboat = moved by the Spirit; Powerboat = powerful or fast progress) Gen. 6:16; 1 Tim. 1:19.

BRAKES - Stop: Hindrance; resist; wait. Acts 16:6-7; 2 Pet. 2:14.

HELICOPTOR - Ministry: Personal; individual; the Church; versatile; stationary (when unmoving). II Tim. 4:2; Rom. 8:14.

MOTORCYCLE - Individual: Personal ministry; independent; rebellion; selfish; pride; swift progress. 2 Pet. 2:10; 1 Sam. 15:23.

PICKUP TRUCK - Work: Personal ministry or natural work. 1 Chron. 13:7; Gal. 6:5.

REARVIEW MIRROR - Word: (Driving backward using the rearview mirror = operating by the letter of the Word instead of by God's Spirit); legalistic; looking back; 2 Cor. 3:6; Gen. 19:26.

RAFT - Adrift: Without direction; aimless; powerless. Eph. 4:14.

TRACTOR - Powerful work: Slow but powerful ministry. Acts 1:8; Acts 4:33.

TRACTOR-TRAILOR - Large burden: Ministry; powerful and/or large work (truck size is often in proportion to the burden or size of the work).

MISCELLANEOUS

ANKLES - Faith: Weak ankles = weak faith; unsupported; undependable. Ezek 47:3.

ARM - Strength or weakness: Savior; deliverer; helper; aid; reaching out. Isa. 52:10; Ps. 136:12.

BANK - Secure: Church; dependable; safe; saved; sure (as in "you can bank on it"); reserved in Heaven. Luke 19:23; Matt. 6:20.

BINOCULARS - Insight: Understanding; prophetic vision; future event. John 16:13; 2 Cor. 3:13, 16.

BLEEDING - Wounded: Hurt, naturally or emotionally; dying spiritually; offended; gossip; unclean. Ps. 147:3; Prov. 18:8.

BLOOD TRANSFUSION - Change: Regeneration; salvation; deliverance. Titus 3:5; Rom. 12:2.

BRIDGE - Faith: Trial; way; joined. Gen. 32:22; 1 Cor. 10:13.

BUTTER - Works: Doing (or not doing) the Word or will of God; deceptive motives; words; smooth. Ps. 55:21; Prov. 30:33.

CALENDAR - Time: Date: event; appointment. Hos. 6:11.

CARDS - Facts: Honesty (as in "putting all your cards on the table"); truth; expose or reveal; dishonest; cheat; deceitful. Rom. 12:17.

CARNIVAL - Worldly: Exhibitionism; divination; competition. Acts 16:16; Luke 21:34.

CHAIR - Position: Seat of authority; rest. Esther 3:1; Rev. 13:2.

CHECK - Faith: The currency of the Kingdom of God; provision; trust. Heb. 11:1; Mark 4:40.

CHOKING - Hinder: Stumbling over something (as in "that's too much to swallow"); hatred or anger (as in "I could choke him!") Mark 4:19.

CHRISTMAS - Gift: Season of rejoicing; spiritual gifts; a surprise; good will. Luke 11:13; 1 Cor. 14:1.

CLOSET - Private: Personal, prayer; secret sin; hidden. Matt. 6:6; Luke 8:17.

COFFEE - Bitter or Stimulant: Repentance; reaping what one has sown; desire for revenge (bitter envying). Num. 9:11; Job 13:26.

DITCH - Habit: Religious tradition; addition; lust; passion. Matt 15:14; Ps. 7:15.

DOMINOES - Continuous: Chain reaction. Lev. 26:37.

EARTHQUAKE - Upheaval: change (by crisis), repentance; trial; God's judgment; disaster; trauma. Acts 16:26; Isa. 29:6.

ECHO - Repetition: Gossip, accusation; voice of many; mocking. Luke 23:21.

EGG - Idea: New thought; plan; promise; potential. Luke 11:12; 1 Tim. 4:15.

FENCE - Barrier: Boundaries; obstacles; religious traditions; doctrines; inhibitions. Gen. 11:6; Jer. 15:20.

GARBAGE (DUMP) - Rejected: Hell; evil; vile; corruption. Mark 9:47-48; 1 Cor. 9:27.

GASOLINE - Fuel: Prayer, inflammatory; gossip; contention; danger. Jude 20; Prov. 26:20-21

GLOVES - Covering: Protection; save; careful (as in "handle with kid gloves"). Ps. 24:3-4; 1 Tim. 4:24-25.

MOWED GRASS - Chastisement: Sickness; financial need or distress; emotional and mental depression or anguish. Amos 7:1-2; 1 Cor. 11:30-32.

GRAVEYARD - Hidden: Past; curse; evil inheritance; hypocrisy; demon. Matt 23:27; Luke 11:44.

GRAVEL PIT - Source: The Word of God; abundant supply. Deut 8:9; 2 Tim. 2:15.

MUDDY ROAD - Flesh: Man's way; lust; passion; temptation; difficulty caused by the weakness of the flesh. Ps. 69:2; Isa. 57:20.

IRONING - Correction: Change; sanctification; exhorting; teaching righteousness; God's discipline; pressure (from trials). Eph. 5:27.

LADDER - Ascend or Descend: Escape; enable; way; steps. Gen. 28:12-13; John 3:13.

LIPS - Words: Seduction; speech. Prov. 7:21; Prov. 10:19.

MAP - Directions: Word of God; correction; advice. Prov. 6:23

MICROPHONE - Voice: Authority; ministry; influence. Matt. 10:27.

MIRROR - Word or one's Heart: God's Word; looking back; memory, past; vanity; Moses' Law. 1 Cor. 13:12; Prov. 27:19.

NEWSPAPER - Announcement: Important event; public exposure; news; gossip. Luke 8:17.

OVEN - Heart: Heat of passion; imagination; meditation; judgment. Hos. 7:6; Ps. 21:9

PAINT BRUSH - Covering: (house painter's brush: regeneration: remodel, renovate; love. Artist's Paint Brush: Illustrative; eloquent; humorous; articulate.) 1 Pet. 4:8; Titus 3:5.

PARACHUTING - Leave: Bail out; escape; flee; saved. 2 Cor. 6:17; Jer. 50:28.

PERFUME - Seduction: Enticement; temptation; persuasion; deception. Prov. 7:7, 10, 13; Eccles. 10:1.

PIE - Whole: Business endeavors; part of the action. Luke 12:13.

PLAY - Worship: Idolatry; covetousness; true worship; spiritual warfare; strife; competition. Col. 3:5; 1 Cor. 9:24.

POSTAGE STAMP - Seal: Authority; authorization; small or seemingly insignificant, but powerful. Esther 8:8; John 6:27.

POT/PAN/BOWL - Vessel: Doctrine; traditions; a determination or resolve; form of the truth; a person. Rom. 2:20; Jer. 1:13.

RADIO - Unchangeable: Unbelief; unrelenting; contentious; unceasing; tradition. Prov. 27:15; Prov. 27:15.

RAILROAD TRACK - Tradition: Unchanging; habit; stubborn; gospel. Mark 7:9, 13; Col. 2:8.

RAPE - Violation: Abuse of authority; hate; desire for revenge; murder. 2 Sam. 13:12, 14-15; Deut 22:25-26.

REFRIGERATOR - Heart: Motive; attitude; stored in heart; harbor. Matt. 12:35; Mark 7:21-22.

ROCKING CHAIR - Old: Past, memories; meditation; retirement; rest. Jer. 6:16.

ROLLER COASTER - Unstable: Emotional instability; unfaithfulness; wavering; manic-depressive; depression; trials; excitement. Isa. 40:4; James 1:6-8.

ROLLER SKATES - Speed: Fast; swift advancement or progress. Rom. 9:28.

ROUND (shape) - Spiritual: (A round face, ring, building, etc) Grace; mercy; compassion; forgiveness. Lev. 19:27.

SEA COAST - Boundary: Flesh (which contains and limits the spirit of man); limitations; weights. Jer. 5:22; Jer. 47:6-7.

SHOVEL - Tongue: Prayer; confession; slander; dig; search; inquire. 2 Kings 3:16-17; Deut. 23:13.

SKIING - Faith: (Water or snowskiing) Supported by God's power through faith; fast progress. John 6:19, 21; Matt 14:29-31.

SLEEP - Unconscious: Unaware; hidden or covered; ignorance; danger; death. Isa. 29:10; Rom. 13:11.

SMILE - Friendly: Kindness; benevolent; without offense; seduction. Prov. 18:24.

SQUARE - Legalistic: (Square eyeglasses, buildings, etc.) Religious or religion; no mercy; hard or harsh; of the world. Lev. 19:9.

SWEEPING - Cleaning: Repentance; change; removing obstacles. 2 Cor. 7:1; 2 Cor. 7:11.

SWIMMING - Spiritual: Serving God; worship; operating the gifts of the Spirit; prophecy. Ezek. 47:5; Eph. 3:8.

FALSE TEETH - Replacement: Wisdom or knowledge gained through experience or previous failures; logical reasoning; tradition. Rom. 5:3-4; Col. 2:8.

TOOTHACHE - Trial: Unfaithful; no faith; unbelief. (Tooth = Wisdom; Ache = Suffering; Broken = Potential pain, i.e. when pressure is applied.) Prov. 25:19.

TELEVISION - Vision: Message; prophecy; preaching; news; evil influence; wickedness. Num. 24:16; Dan. 2:19.

THUNDER - Change or Without Understanding: (Of what the Spirit is saying or of the signs of the times). Dispensational change (i.e., a change in the way God deals with His people); warning of impending judement or trouble. John 12:28-29; Ps. 18:13.

TITLE/DEED - Ownership: Authorization; possession. Gen. 23:20.

TREE STUMP - Unbelief; roots; tenacious; obstacle; immovable; hope. Job 14:7-9.

URINATING - Spirit: Full bladder = Pressure. Compelling urge; temptation (such as sexual lust or strife); Bladder Infection or Cancer = Offence: Enmity. Prv.o 17:14.

WASHCLOTH - Truth: Doctrine; understanding. (Dirty cloth = False doctrine: Insincere apology; error.) Ps. 51:7; Job 14:4.

WATERMELON - Fruit: The fruit of good or evil works; the pleasures of sin. (Seeds = Words; Water = Spirit; Sweetness = Strength; Green = Life; Red = Passion; Yellow = Gifts) Num. 11:5; Prov. 1:31.

WESTERN - Frontier: ("The wild west," a western movie, etc.) Pioneer, spiritual warfare; boldness; challenge. Deut. 20:10; Josh. 3:4.

Additional Resources by
James W. & Michal Ann Goll

Prophetic Encounters

Featuring James W. Goll
Music by John Belt

Be prepared to receive a Prophetic Encounter as James W. Goll shares stories, and personal experiences, reads scripture and releases prayers of impartation. Titles include: Beautiful, Bread of His Presence, Rock the Nations, Over Here, Dread Champions, Giants of Faith, Days of Acceleration, The Golden Anointing, and many more...

$15.00

The Healing Presence

Featuring James W. & Michal Ann Goll
Music by John Belt

Receive God's Healing Presence as James W. & Michal Ann Goll read scripture, share stories, and release prayers of impartation. "The Lord really visited us in this recording!" Titles include: The Hem of His Garment, The Day of Healing, How Lovely, The Healing River, and many more...

$15.00

Invitation To Intimacy

This CD was professionally recorded at the Wagner Leadership Institute as James W. Goll was caught up into another realm. It contains over 60 minutes of prophetic, spontaneous worship and teaching with keyboard and instrumentation with John Belt. Soak with this one!

$15.00

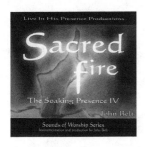

Sacred Fire

by John Belt

This non-stop instrumental CD will take you on a journey with many creative sounds. The sacred fire is fire that burns in our lives before God in prayer. Songs include Waters of Moriah, Sacred Fire, Celestial Door, Heaven's Shores and others . . .

$15.00

For Additional Products by James W. and Michal Ann Goll

Visit www.jamesgoll.com | Call 1~877~200~1604

Study Guides by James W. Goll

Over the years, James W. Goll has taught these practical tools to help people all over the world learn a prophetic lifestyle. The comprehensive study guides in this series can be used either for individual study or with a class or small group. Following each detailed lesson are simple questions for reflection. As you work through these lessons, you will be inspired to take your place in God's prophetic army.

Equipping in the Prophetic / Enlisting a Prophetic Army

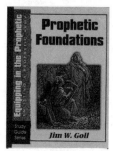

Prophetic Foundations
The first of this series on the prophetic. These 12 lessons include:
For the Many - Not the Few, The History of the Prophetic,
Intimacy in the Prophetic, Power & Perils of the Prophetic Spirit
Seven Expressions of the Prophetic Spirit, Prophesy Life,
The Prophetic Song of the Lord, and more...

$15.00

Experiencing Dreams & Visions
This is the second Guide in the series. These 12 lessons include:
God's Multi-faceted Voice, Visionary Revelation, Journaling,
Tools For Interpreting Revelation, Dream Language,
Receiving and Judging Revelation, Wisdom in Handling Revelation,
Dream Language I & II, Tips for Interpratations , and more...

$15.00

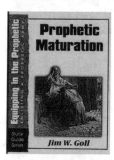

Prophetic Maturation
This is the third Guide in the series. These 12 lessons Include:
Called Into Character, From Character to Commissioning,
Seizing your Prophetic Destiny Parts 1 & 2, The Cross -
The Prophetic Lifestyle, Four levels of Prophetic Ministry,
The Seer and the Prophet: Similarities and Differences, and more...

$15.00

Understanding Supernatural Encounters
This is the fourth Guide in the series. These 12 lessons Include:
Keys to the Supernatural, How to Receive Revelation,
Demonstrating Three Models, The Deception of the Anointing,
Levels Of Supernatural Visions Parts 1 & 2, Trances Defined,
Ministry and Function of Angels, Current Day Accounts of Angelic
Activity, and more...

$15.00

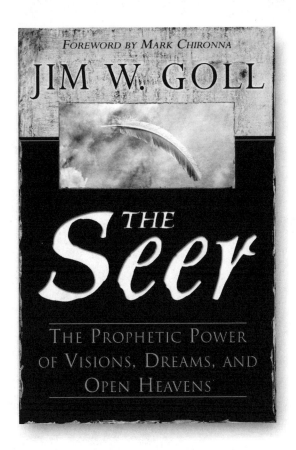

THE SEER

The prophetic movements in church history and in contemporary life are fed by two mighty streams: the prophet, whose revelation is primarily verbal, and the seer, whose revelation is more visionary in nature. While the role of the prophet is familiar, less is known about the seer dimension. To many people, these visionary prophets remain mysterious, otherworldly, and even strange.

Knowledge dispels misunderstanding. Join author Jim W. Goll on an exciting and insightful journey into this lesser-known dimension—the visionary world of the seer. You will discover the prophetic power of dreams, visions, and life under the open heavens.

ISBN 0-7684-2232-9

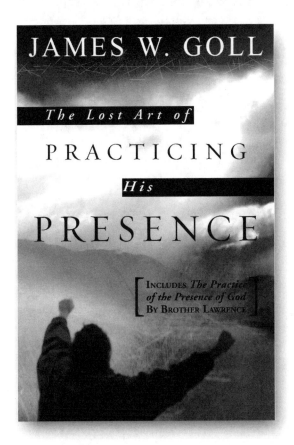

THE LOST ART OF PRACTICING HIS PRESENCE

The presence of God is meant to be more than just an occasional event during Sunday morning Worship—you are meant to live in God's presence! In The Lost Art of Practicing His Presence, James W. Goll uncovers ancient and nearly forgotten keys to deeper intimacy with Christ Jesus while revealing the ease of working with Christ instead of for Him.

Through this book you will rediscover the lost precepts of Biblical meditation, contemplative prayer, and waiting on the Lord and learn how to apply them in your own life. Most importantly, you will gain inspiration for your own intimate walk and the courage to spread the fire His presence to everyone around you!

ISBN 0-7684-2322-8